FIFTY ESSAYS

Prof. SHRINIVAS

Mehta Publishing House

FIFTY ESSAYS by Prof. SHRINIVAS
Email : author@mehtapublishinghouse.com
© Mehta Publishing House

Publisher   : Mehta Publishing House
                    1941, Sadashiv Peth, Madiwale Colony,
                    Pune 411030. INDIA

Cover Design   : Suhas Chavan

Publishing Date : 1973 / August, 1997 / March, 2000 / January, 2002 /
                    July, 2007 / July, 2013 / March, 2020

P Book ISBN 9788177662702
E Book ISBN   9789353174408

E Books available on : play.google.com/store/books
                    www.amazon.in

INDEX

ESSAYS AND ESSAY - WRITING

1. What is an essay ?

The literal meaning of the word essay is a trial or an attempt. So, It comes to mean some attempt at writing on a set subject. This will make it clear that an essay can never be a complete or a detailed treatment of any subject. By its nature itself, it is imperfect and unfinished. It is this original meaning which the writers of essays must always keep in their mind. If they do so, they will easily lose their fear of the essay and the art of essay - writing.

If the essay is really so simple and imperfect, why is it honoured as a form of literature and is supposed to be very difficult to write ?

Some explanation on this topic will help to clear, the treatment of the subject. The essay was taken up by French and English writer of great literary merit and used for expressing their own likes, dislikes, experiences, observations and even advice. Thus, little by little, the essay lost its original idea of trial and attempt and developed into a form of prose writing having some element of fine style, interest in personality and sometimes even the interest of a character sketch or a short story. Great writers from the 16th to 20th century have written such fine essays which have now become a permanent part and parcel of literature in prose.

However, when students in school and college are asked to write an essay in their examination, nobody expects them to write a literary essay like that of Bacon, Addison or Gardiner (great essayists). What the examiner wants to see is whether the student can write a short piece of composition in prose from about two or three hundred to five hundred words on a given subject in simple but clear and correct English. To avoid a confusion between the literary and the school and college essay (the two different meanings and functions) now a days, the word essay is dropped from the question papers of examinations from S. S. C. to B. A. In its place, the instructions are to write ' a continuous composition or a prose narrative', Sometimes, the question even says, 'Write 40 to 50 lines on any one of the following subjects.' However, what the examiner has in his mind is the essay, not of the literary, but of the school and college type.

From this discussion, the students can form a clear idea of what they have got to do when they take up this question of essay or continuous composition or even that of writing 40 to 50 lines on a subject. They should not run away with the idea that they can write anything they like in these thirty to forty lines. What they write must have some thought, some plan, some arrangement behind it. This can be easily done if the student studies the subject systematically and writes the essay, systematically, point by point, step by step.

Nearly all the failures in essay - writing are due to the reason that the writer takes up a subject without thinking properly about it and begins to write at once, whatever comes to his mind without having any idea of the proper arrangement or an effective ending. That is why some times the student writes a paragraph or two and then finds that he has no further material to write on that subject. He has to cross out what he has witten and to begin to write on some other subject from the beginning. The result is a kind of hasty, disorderly and confused piece of writing without any good beginning or an affective ending. So, the first step in successful essay - writing is the choice of a proper subject. One should choose only that subject about which one has some stock of material (thought, examples etc.). The second test of a proper subject would be that of personal interest. In the examination, there are no less than five of six subjects given for choice. The writer should read all these and ask himself in which of these he has some particular interest and if possible some kind of experience.

It is a rule in all writing, whether literary or in school and college, that unless one is really interested in some writing, that writing can never be really interesting and attractive to others. There will always be atleast one subject in which the writer can take some interest and write with some degree of enthusiasm and interest. If this is done, and if there is enough material in the mind, one will never be cought in the position of feeling dried up and being forced to cross out what he has written!

2. Gathering the material

The commonest complaint of all students (When they are asked to write an essay) is that they have no material to put in the essay and that they do not know what they can write about. This complaint is really quite false and is based on a complete misunderstanding. As we have said above, a student is not expected to pack all knowledge of a particular subject in his essay. The reader or the examiner does not want to learn anything from the writer of the essay. All he wants to see is whether the writer has a few ordinary ideas about the subject and whether he is able to express his ideas in a correct English and arrange these in proper order, surely, this is not a difficult task.

But what about the material? As we have said, it is a wrong idea to suppose that one has no material to write about. Any student who has come to the level of S. S. C. or the college classes has enough knowledge and material' in his head to write dozen and dozens of essays. The pity of it is that no one has taught him how to bring out that material out of his head and to make a proper use of it for writing of any essay.

It is like having a big sealed tin of food or milk and going hungry because one has no tine-opener or cannot ope n that tin so as to bring out the food for eating.

In the following lines we shall give such a tin opener' to the students so that they can open the sealed tin of their mind and can take out the thoughtmaterial to write an essay on any subject of their choice.

Some readers may think this reference to 'mental tin openers' as being rather fianciful and even nonsense. So to assure them we note that the phrase ' mental tin openers' and the method we give below has the authority of a well known writer named T.W.H.Warner and the method given is as recommended in his book on essay writing called 'the Writing of English.' These mental tin openers are the interrogative pronouns and other questions which aim at making the mind work to give an answer to the questions. To change the figure of speech, these questions are like taps of water. You just turn on one tap and a stream of ideas will follow. When it stops, you can turn on the other tap and gather the ideas from it. These ideas should then be rapidly noted down in pencil and will form the raw material of which the essay is to be produced. These interrogative expressions are the following :-

What-who-where-how so-how not so-why so-why not so-etc.

Of course, these words are not a magic charm which will write an essay for you. They must not be repeated mechanically. They should be given a serious trial if they are to show any result. Merely making fun of these will lead to nothing. Let us take a very common and popular subject and show how these questions will provide a lot of material for writing a good-length essay on it. It should be noted that we are not refferring to any technical or out of the way knowledge but simply putting down the ideas which are present in the mind of any ordinary student S. S. C. level upwards.to the graduate class level.

The subject is Strikes (which is an important subject always given for essay writing to students.) *What* : What do you mean by a strike? The literal meaning and the meaning when the workers go on a strike. What do they do ? What is the use of strikes ?

When : Put down the various occasions when strikes take place (when there is no bonus, no enough payment, when there is injustice, cruelty etc.).

Where : Note all the places where strike takes place-Factories, mines, offices, schools and other institutions.

Why : Note the motives or reasons why strikes are resorted to (for justice, for fair treatment, for housing, for transport, for higher wages, for removal of officers who are cruel, corrupt or unfair etc.).

How : How are the strikes managed and carried out? serving of notice, picketing, processions, publicity, gathering of funds, sending representatives to the government, the factory owners, meetings for compromise, ending the strike etc.

Who : Note the various kinds of people who go on strikes (factory workers, miners, teachers, domestic servants, students, also note who are *not* allowed to go on strikes, the policemen, the soldiers, the sailors, men in essential services in communist countries etc.)

Why so : Why are strikes allowed, why are they justified or necessary.

Why not so : Why certain kinds of strikes should not be allowed (e.g. those getting a salary of hundreds and thousands and stiM wanting more. When there is already a machinery for settling disputes like arbitration etc.).

The reader will feel that the material is more than enough for an essay and yet there is nothing in it which any fairly intelligent student does not know. All these are mere ideas. They must not be left as they are. Each fact, each idea can be supported and illustrated by an incident or fact wich one has read in some newspaper, story, novel, picture. In short, the raw material of an essay is every thing which one thinks of, hears, reads or sees around him. The essay should then be brought to a close with a concluding paragraph in which the writer gives his own opinion, view or experience. We have written in detail about the writing of reflective or expository essays (meaning the essays which are based on some thoughtful subjects and those which explain some subjects). There are simpler kind of essays like the descriptive essays, narrative essays, personal essays in which all this effort for getting material will not be required at all.

3. Descriptive essay

In this kind of essay, the writer has to describe some interesting scene or place or person that he has seen (e.g. a moonlight walk, a burning house, the sea-side, some machine, pet animal etc.)

Narrative essay : In this form, the student is asked to write an account of some incident or happening from the beginning to the end of that incident or action (e.g. a riot, a street fight, a picnic, the life of some great man, some festival, a social gathering, an incident in your life etc.).

4. Personal essay

Most of the artistic and literary essays belong to this type. In it, the writer has to express his own likes, dislikes, opinions, doubts, suggestions etc. on any given subject. In one way, this is easy enough because one has only to write freely what one thinks and feels about a subject and about one's own experiences. But from the other point of view it is the»most difficult type of essay to write and to make it sufficiently interesting. That is because the interest of a personal essay lies in the interest and importance of the person who is writing about himself. If your personality has nothing interesting in it but is dull and common-place, the personal essay will be also dull and common place. In addition, a personal essay demands some element of style, freshness of approach and some humour. So, this form of essay can be best treated by those who are confident that they have some of these qualities and qualifications. For others, the remaining types of essay will be safer.

In general, the descriptive and narrative essays are expected from students of the S.S.C. and P.D. level. Reflective as well as narrative and personal essays are expected from the students of the graduate class (S.Y. & T. Y. level)

We shall sum up the discussion by giving twelve practical hints for essay writing, step by step. We are confident that any student who follows these rules carefully and systematically and practises writing regularly will find no difficulty in writing good and readable essays.

5. Hints on essay-writing

1) Understand the full meaning, limit and scope of each subject (given for eslay writing) clearly in your mind. Then select the subject about which you know most, and in which you feel really interested. Never write on a subject about whose meaning you are not sure. ' :

2) Think over the selected subject and ask yourself some questions to gather information about it. Write down what your mind tells you in 'answer to th'e following questions one by one : what, when, why, where, who, why so, why not so, how so, when so, where so, where not so, etc.

3) The answers which you get from the points form the raw material for your essay. Put down these first in pencil and then arrange them in a logical order.

4) Now fit these points with proper examples, incidents, references, current incidents etc.

5) With this material now make a synopsis or a rough outline and check it with the points to see that nothing is left out.

6) Now (and not before it) begin to write the essay closely following the outline and keeping the following instructions in mind.

7) Every essay should have an introduction (one paragraph), main body (two to three paragraphs) and conclusion (one short paragraph).

8) Keep the introduction short, arresting and enter into the subject at once. Do not start with a definition and do not go too far back before entering into the subject.

9) The main body of the essay should contain arguments or incidents or fittting illustrations to go with the ideas of arguments. Do not write only in the abstract, vague and general terms. Use concrete words and always give examples in support of your arguments.

10) The conclusion should be brief and effective. The essay should end by showing and proving what the writer started to do at the begining. Do not summarize what you have already written in the essay.

11) The style of writing should be clear, concrete and grammatically correct. Avoid long and rambling sentences (because they often lead to mistakes). Pay particular attention to the use of articles.

12) Never submit the essay hastily before revising thoroughly and correcting all the mistakes of spelling, and grammar and before checking dates, facts, names and references for their correctness.

■ ■ ■

Stage I (Lower)
Descriptive and narrative essays.

1. A Street Fight

Every one must have watched a street fight in a village, town or city. Such fights always attract a big crowd though they often lead to a riot or a fight among even the spectators. There is some thing in these fights which appeals to some feeling which is hidden deep into the minds of everybody. That is why every one finds a street fight so interesting.

I myself has such an experience the other day as I saw sitting in the gallery of my house, one cyclist coming fast from the east and another cyclist . coming by a cross road. Some how it seemed that the brakes of one of the cyclists had failed and so instead of stopping, he dashed, against the other cycle. Both the cyclists fell down on the ground but neither of them seemed to be seriously hurt. I thought that both of them would perhaps get up, brush their clothes and go by their way with perhaps a few words of blame or anger.

However, I was surprised to see that one of the cyclists caught the other (younger one) by the collar and began to abuse him loudly for his carelessness. The other cyclist tried to argue and even to refer the matter to the police, but the first cyclist gave him a blow and a slap in the' face. By this time, a crowd of passers-by had gathered round the two men and some persons were trying to separate the two. But the first cyclist seemed to get more and more angry and started to hit and kick not only the younger cyclist but even the person who was trying to control him! It was a strange thing to see how a new fight now began between, the first man and the man controlling him. In this confusion, the second cyclist quickly raised up his cycle and slipped away without being noticed.

Now began the second act of the fight with some friends on the side of both the fighters adding to the noise and confusion. The simple street fight now seemed to be on the point of growing into a regular riot. Fortunately, a passing policeman entered into the crowd and caught hold of the first cyclist. He blew his whistle and two other policemen came running and took away the cyclist and the man he was fighting with. The crowd gradually dispersed. The sight made me think how easily the people (who seem to be calm and quiet) suddenly lose their control of the mind and rush into a fight in the street.

■　■

2. Street Hawkers

A street hawker is a man who sells goods of common use from door to door or on the street. Such hawkers have now become very common in city life.. Some of them carry portable stands to keep their goods and remain standing at corners "of the streets. Some spread their goods on the footpath. Some carry things on trays hanging from their necks. Some sell their things in railway compartments and move from one carriage to another.

Some people wonder why persons buy things from hawkers when there are so many shops in towns and even in villages. But though there are shops, hawkers still find customers because they satisfy certain needs of the people more easily.

Hawkers often sell things like vegetables, eatables etc. cheaper than the things in big shops. That is because they have not to pay any rent for shops or to pay wages to servants, pay for light and municipal taxes. So they can afford to sell things at a rather cheaper rate. However the buyers have to be rather careful in purchasing things from the hawkers because one cannot often return the goods to a hawker as one can return things to a shop.

It is interesting to watch how a typical hawker uses various ways to persuade the people to buy his goods. In a city, there is almost a continuous stream of hawkers throughout the day, each one selling different things at different times of the day and the season. Early in the morning, there is a cry of newspaper hawkers. Then comes a woman hawker shouting the names of various vegetables and shouting at the top of her voice that they are all quite fresh and quite cheap. She is very popular especially among the housewives in various flats, in the houses and colonies which are at a distance from the central vegetable market. . ..

After her, there are other hawkers, some selling bread and biscuits, sweets for children. There are salesmen selling toilet goods asking for waste paper, old bottles etc. During the afternoon, when men are away, there are hawkers who sell cut pieces of cloth for the ladies and toning and mending vessels. They always attract many women in the houses and flats all round. In the evening there are hawkers selling hot articles for refreshment and they also find a welcome from tfusy housewives and others who have no desire or energy to prepare fresh things for refreshment. Late in the evening, again there are other hawkers selling different kinds of fruits, scented-sticks (joss-stocks) and other things. Late at night, there is a call from a solitary man carrying bottles of oil offering to massage the tired businessmen.

Thus, the hawkers are of all kinds, ages and sell all kinds of goods and services. A proverb says "It takes all sorts of people to make to world." So, Even the hawkers have a part to play in city life because they satisfy demand of the society.

■ ■

3. A moonlight walk

A writer has remarked that going for a walk is one of the pleasantest things in life. One would like to add that such walk becomes even more enjoyable if it is taken on a moon-lit night. Some people prefer to walk and to run in the morning for exercise. Some old men go for a walk in the evening for their health. But a walk in the moonlight is undertaken for the joy of it.

It is a matter of surprise and delight to see how even ordinary things and places appear strange and beautiful in the moonlight. Ugly, dark and broken buildings, houses and huts appear beautiful and romantic when they are seen from a distance in the moonlight. Common trees appear to have strange shapes with their shadows. A river appears like a stream of liquid silver while the sea appears to be like a vast flowing white silk sheet moving up and down. Even the cows and dogs lying asleep in the street appear strange. An English poet named De La Mare has written a small beautiful poem called ' Silver'. In it, he describes how moonlight turns-even the common and ugly things around us into silver.

A walk in a moonlight is the best way of bringing peace and harmony in one's mind. All around lies peace while one sits in some 'open plain or on some small hill. The peace is disturbed only by some distant sounds like those of the bark of a dog or a rumbling of a motor lorry passing at a distance. It is very pleasant to lie on the grass and to watch the moon slowly seeming to pass through the sky. The clouds pass across the face of the moon and give an appearance of the motion to the moon. One can look at the dark shape apperantly like that of a deer or a hare on he face of the moon and can wonder where the American space travellers had landed on the moon. Now, every educated person knows abouf'ᶜSiie mountains on the moon and about the visits of the space travellers to the moon. This has taken away something from the mystery and romance of the moon no doubt. But the cool and pleasant moonlight is still as refreshing and soothing as it was in the past. Indeed, even a worried and unhappy man will feel somewhat comforted and at peace, when he returns home after a walk in the moonlight, either by himself or in the company of someone whom he likes or loves.

■ ■

4. A fable you like best

Many fables tell interesting stories about men and animals and also point out some truth about human life. The fables of the old Greek slave Aesop are known all ever the world and have been read by generations of children for hundreds of years. Among these fables, I like the following very much.

Aesop describes how the statue or idol of some God or saint was to be carried to a town. The sculptor (or the artist who had made that statue) packed it carefully and placed it on the back of a horse. As he came near the city, many people came forward to recieve this horse. They placed garlands of flowers round his neck and all over his back. They gave him grass and water and scattered flowers over the path on which it had to walk. Then came some bands of musicians who went on playing sweet music as the procession walked on to the temple. Some girls, finely dressed, came forward to receive the procession and sang and danced in front of the horse carrying the images. Someone would come out of a house and offer some food to the horse and would scatter flowers over him. The horse saw how people on both sides bowed their heads and folded their hands in salutation as the horse passed through the lines of people on both sides of the road.

All this praise, respect and offerings began to mak'e the horse feel the very proud. He began to think that his master had never shown any real interest in him though he had a great value. He felt that only the people in the town had really appreciated his greatness. He determined to teach his master a lesson by running away from him at the first opportunity.

As he was thinking in this manner, he came to the newly built temple. The priests came forward to take the statue down from the back of the horse. They carried it with great respect inside the temple and everybody followed them. The horse was left all alone outside. He felt this to be an insult and tried to enter the temple by pushing some people aside. To his shock and surprise, some of these people now began to speak very roughly to him. One or two men even took up sticks and began to beat him. Finally, they drove him out of the temple-yard with kicks and abuses for .his arrogance. At last, the poor horse knew that all the honour and attention he had received was not due to his merit. It was the result of the statue placed on his back. When it was gone, no one had any interest for him.

This fable about the foolish horse can teach a lesson even to the men who occupy some high position for the time being and find people to be so respectful towards them. It is the power and authority which the people,respect, and not the man.

■ ■

5. A good neighbour

Man is a social animal. A part of his happiness depends on his neighours and his neighbourhood. Good neighbours can add to the comfort and happiness of a family while bad nighbours can make a family miserable. Perhaps that is why the Bible asked a Christian to 'love thy neighbour as thyself". It is an advice which is however rather difficult tc follow in practice though easy and attractive in theory.

Anyone will be able to give examples of bad neighbours who borrow things and never return them, who make a lot of noice when you want peace and quiet. They are never around when some help is needed, but will come unasked a-d never leave others free when there is something interesting in one's house.

No doubt, such cases of indifference, selfishness and even of deliberate mischief can be found here and there among the neighbours. However, there are far more cases in which groups of people live in a friendly atmosphere and co-operation. This is far more common among the poor people who live in huts, and rooms in chawls than among those rich men who live in ownership flats and bungalows. Any one of the poor families will tell you how the neighbours were of great help when someone in the family fell sick or had an accident. Occasions like the marriage, death the funeral etc. are the occassions when help from a neighbour is greatly appreciated. One must always be ready to be good neighbour to others just as one expects others to be a good and . *i* helpful neighbours. There is a very touching story in the Bible about a man who can be called a (real) neighbour u:; vsho does not deserve to be called one.

A man was attacked and robbed by some thieves. As he lay wounded on the road, several people from his neighbourhood saw him lying there, but went away without helping him. Then a man from a different place saw him and dressed his wounds and made arrangements for his nursing and recovery. Christ then asked who among these people could be called the real neighbour of that man. The story suggests therefore that a real neighbour is not the man who only lives near another, but one who helps others in times of need and takes interest in their. company. Happy are those who have such neighbours, in the real sense of the word, around them.

6. Early morning in a city

Poets have written very beautifully about early morning on the sea, the rivers, mountains etc. But early morning even in cities has its own beauty. It must be experienced and seen, personally, before it can be appreciated. In the city, we cannot see the sun coming up over the hills or the sea, yet we can see the gradual reddening of the eastern sky even behind the buildings. The best place from which we can see the beauty of the morning in a city will be from the top of some tall building. From the top, we can see the eastern sky, first very dark, then faintly dark, then gray and then faint rosy in colour. This pale rose then becomes orange and finally bright red. Then the first rays of the sun come out almost in straight lines and begin to turn the tops of temples, buildings, theatres etc. into gold. The light gradually spreads out until the dark outlines of buildings begin to come out in their natural and familiar shape of every day life.

At first the doors and windows of houses are all closed like the eyes of persons who are fast asleep. So, the poet (Wordsworth) gives out a natural exclamation- "Dear God, the very houses seem asleep." Like the houses, the streets too seem almost assleep during the late night. Gradually, the first milk cars and trucks carrying cans and bottles of milk begin to rumble through the streets. The street now wakes up and from our place at the top, we can see the winking and passing headlights of the trucks, private cars and the early buses in big cities.

The beauty of the early morning in the city is therefore not the beauty of hills and flowers, trees and birds as in open air scenes of nature. In cities, even the human element has its own beauty, at least in early morning. We see' the early housewife coming out and sprinkling some water before the doorstep and sketching patterns in red and white chalk powder. We hear the faint devotional songs of some old men and women before their songs are drowned by the mecehanical music of radios which come into life at six o' clock. Even the workers returning from the late night shift in mills and others going out for their early shift form groups ar.d formations in streets which have their appeal to a sympathetic spectaror. Gradually, the city begins to hum and the sounds grow louder and louder like some huge machine which gradually begins to run faster and makes a sound louder and louder. It is morning and the huge machine of human activity in the city life has begun. But the beauty of the early morning still remains behind in our mind like some faint perfume.

■　■

7. Late night in a city

Night life in big cities is often too bright and noisy, for the people who love a life of peace and quiet. But e. en such people will find the late night in a city more comforting and peaceful if they come out to have a walk or happen to return from some journey late at night. The brightly burning lamps and lightings of cinema theatres, hotels, irig shops go out one by one. Darkness gradually comes rolling in. It is pierced only by the lamps on the public greets. All around these, there is perfect darkness. The streets are all deserted with the exception of some occasional bicycle of a man returning home after the night shift in some factory or some long distance truck roaring through the empty streets, Such unusual quietness in the streets produces a sensation of peace though some times a feeling of fear also passes through the mind when one sees some dark figure walking through the shadows in a suspicious manner.

The late night in a city brings out quite a new variety of persons whom one seldom meets during the day time. Many of these are undesirable characters though some of them deserve pity rather than anger and punishment. Such are the poor beggers who are moving about in search of some place of rest in a dark but sheltered corners. Thieves and robbers find this time of the night most suitable for their profession. The men who have seen better days but have come down in life remain hidden during the day, but come out for a walk late at night when there is no danger of someone recognizing them.

I made this strange discovery when I accidentally met a friend whom I had long supposed to be either dead or departed from the city. As I walked home from railway station after a journey very late one night, I suddenly caught sight of a person in torn clothes with an over-grown beard walking along wih bent shoulders. As I looked at his face, I gave a start to find that he was my long lost friend. At first, he was too proud to acknoledge that he was the person for whom I called. But after some time, he answered me and then told me his tale of woe, disappointment and failure in life. Now he was working at some part time, job which paid hardly enough to keep his body and soul together. He moved out very late at night to avoid his creditors and his prosperous friends who had all refused to help him in his hours of need. He was however too proud to accept any charity or help from me and moved away into darkness silently, like a shadow. Such are the scenes of a city late at night. They leave an impression of some lonely and sad feeling on the mind which one cannot however really account for.

■ ■

8. My Village

Every person has one dearest memory in his life though he may go any where in the world. It is the memory of the place where he was born and where he spent his early days. Those born in a city do not have as warm a place for it in their heart, as those who come from a village ha\ e. I recently came to know this when I found my friend in tears one day as he remembered his native village far i'.vay from the city where he lived. He described it to me with great affection in detail as follows.

It is a village with a hill at the back and the sea in front of it. As you enter the village, you see a small temple surrounded by a few trees. The village has only one main - treet with a few shops on both sides. But small groups of hut-like houses lie scattered on both sides of the road. The people in the village are still grouped together, according to their castes or professions even when such differences are being forgotten in city life. However, there is not much difference in the houses or standard of living in these men of different cases and professions. The best house is that of the village money-lender and after that of the landlord. All the rest are mostly huts with roofs of cocconut leaves, a oven together to form a roof.

There is neither piped water nor any modern way of sanitation and lighting (of electricity) in such a small village. Wells for drinking water are found here and there and all the people share the water peacefully. A big tank serves for the purpose of washing clothes while most people bathe either in he sea or in the water drawn from the wells. There is very little of industry in the village. The two main activities are those of farming and of fishing. Rice fields lie outside the village and many men have cocconut and mango trees of their own. A group of fishermen go out regularly in their beats for fishing. However, there are no facilities for transport of fish or for their preservation. So, it is not a profitable business. It just keeps their body and soul together.

Though the men are poor, they live a life a quite ease if not of great happiness. Men of different c;rr. rn_nities and even of religions live here peacefully and c:-;rerate in the work of a Village Panchayat. They come together on the occasion of some festival. Occasions of joy like marriage and of sorrow like a funeral show how these people can come together as good neighbours and share their joy and sorrows. However, such villages are now getting fewer, as s most young men in the village are turning towards towns and cites for employment. Soon, such lonely far off. small villages will have only the old men and women together in their houses which they do not want to 'er e Mke the young people.

■ ■

9. An animal you like most

Every person likes the animal most suited to his nature. Those who like a life a activity and adventure admire lions, tigers, hunting-dogs and horses. Girls usually like birds more than animals. Those who live in the village natural!;, like the bulls and cows, sheep and goats as they are most useful for them and are found every where around them. Men and women of fastion have a liking for dogs of fancy and foriegn breed like the Alsetian dogs, the fox-terriers or the small lap and toy dogs often seen in a company of actresses etc.

I myself have a liking for a cat. This might appear to be rather a strange choice but I have my own reasons. A cat is a gentle, clean and quiet animal. It does net make a nuisance of itself, nor is a source of danger like a dog. It has a gift of being noiseless in its movements and of becoming almost invisible when it hides in some corner or under some covering. However its presence in a house as pleasing as well as comforting. It likes the company of people and knows that the people also love it.

The most attractive stage in the life of a cat is its early stage when it is like a small ball of fur called a kitten. It runs about the house, playing with little bits of paper and can play with a ball of wool or string for hours together. It jumps, it runs, and it hides in various places all by itself, without any reason. It is merely the activity which it enjoys. It is the new life which it is discovering.

A grown up male cat is however seldom very attractive. It has something of the pride and cruelty of a little tiger. But female cats continue to be gentle, quiet and peaceful throughout their lives. The soft purring sound made by a cat when it lovingly rubs itself by your legs while asking milk makes one's heart go out to this gentle creature.

Even from the practical point of view, a cat is a very useful creature in the house. It keeps the house free from mice, rats, insects, and even from serpents. It is a creature that loves cleanlyness and spends hours lying in the sun cleaning its body from the neck down to the tip of its tail using its soft pink tongue as a cleaning brush.

One wonders why some people dislike and hate cats calling them cunning and crafty. It is an insult to a cat when girls use the term ' cat' in contempt for some cunning and crafty girl. No doubt, the cat loves its home more than the owner of the home and remains behind even when the owner leaves the house. A cat has a spirit of independence and is never slavish and humble before its owner like a dog. It can use it sharp nail and teeth if some one is over-familiar with it. Thus, it keeps its own dignity. Lastly, a cat has the sense not to trouble its owner even at the time of its death. It usually leaves the house and goes and dies in some corner, far away from the house. Is it then any wonder that I like and love cats.?

10. The Autobiography of a book

I have a habit of visiting a weekly market where many old things are sold. I am particularly fond of visiting the shops on the footpath where heaps of old books are exposed for sale. The prices of new books have risen so high now, that it is very difficult and almost impossible- for people of the middle class to buy new books. However, one can often get a second-hand book in the old market for quarter of the price of a book or even less. For some limes, I wanted to buy a book of the complete plays of Shakespeare, but the price was beyond my- reach. So, 1 was always on the look out for that book in the old marker Imagine my joy when last week, I saw that book in a heap of old books. The cover of the book was missing •but all Ihe plays and poems of Shakespeare were present. The Shopkeeper paid more attention to the binding and the coiulilion of the books than to their content. So, it was a pleasanl shock to me when he demanded only 75 Paisas for that book. 1 was quite ready to pay the price but jusl to take a chance, I offered 50 Paisas and the shopkeeper carelessly lossed the book in front of me. I caught it at once and quickly left the shop after paying my 50 Paisa coin. I was afraid that the shopkeeper might withdraw his offer!

I spent an hour at night in repairing the torn and loose pages and in putting a good and clean binding after covering it with cloth and thick paper. I kept it under a big weight to dry and went to sleep with great satisfaction. Imagine my surprise when that night I had a strange dream in which I saw that book in its fine leather binding and gold coloured edges and letters on its back. What is stranger is the fact that the book seemed to be speaking to me and I found nothing extra-ordinary in the fact. The book opened and words seem to come out of it some what with the following matter.

"My boy, I am very glad that you have purchased me and have tried to restore me to my former condition. But alas! I can never regain my original beauty, I was made and printed in England and was sent to India along with other great books of literature. For many years, I lived comfortably in the private library of my owner who was a great lover of literature. Unfortunately, after his death, his son simply made a heap of the books on the floor and sold the fine teakwood cupboard. Children in the house tore away my fine binding to use it as a container for their notebooks. After a week, a merchant in the old bazaar bought all the books for a small sum and threw me on the footpath. I felt great sorrow at my lot and was very angry to find that these priceless plays were worth only 50 Paisas in the old market. I hope you will at/ east get me well bound and keep me with you with the due honour. "

At this stage, I woke up and lovingly and reaspectfully took up that book. I made a solemn resolve to get it bound in the best manner and to give it a place of honour in my collection of books.

■   ■

11. The life of a great Patriot

Modern India can boast of many great patriots. Among all these great men, the greatest name is that of Gandhiji, the father of free India. It was under his leadership that the people of India carried out a non-voilent struggle for freedom for many years and finally won their freedom in 1947. It will be interesting to review the outstanding career of Gandhiji as a lover of truth, justice, service and freedom.

Mohandas Karamchand Gandhi was born on the 2nd of October, 1869. He came from a prominent and well-placed family in Saurashtra. The early life of Gandhiji has been freely and frankly described by Gandhiji himself in the story of his own life. Gandhiji tells us that he was neither strong nor very clever. However, he loved truth from his childhood and was very devoted to his parents. After passing his matriculation examination (now called S.S.C.) Gandhiji was sent to England to be a Barrister. He had several interesting experiences in England and returned as a Barrister to India. By nature, he was not fit to work for money or worldy success. He visited South Africa on business. Here he became interested in the problem of the Indians in South Africa and gradually became a leader of the Indians in the struggle for their human rights. It was here that he formed his famous philosophy of *Satyagraha* or non-violent non co-operation. To the end of his life, he firmly beleived that the struggle for rights carried on peacefully, without hate for the opponent and with a willingness for sacrifice would a!\va\s succeed. And the wonder was that even the strong and pitiless South African Government came to terms with Gandhi;! and agreed to remove the unjust laws against the Indian people.

Gandhiji returned to India and took o\ er the control of the struggle for Indian independence after the death of Lokamanya Tilak. His selfless devotion to his idea, the purity and honesty of his life gradually collected a group of patriots who were inspired by his ideal and his personality. Gandhiji established his famous Sabarmati Ashrama to train the leaders for Satyagraha and sent them to various parts of the country.

The struggle against the British started under his

leadership from 1930 right up to the 'Quit India' movement in 1942 and continued till independence of India frnalh in 1947. The movement had many ups and downs, hopes and disappointments; but ended in success. Even after independence, Gandhiji carried on his work of national service, peace and harmony among the people without earring for an\ post of power. He was unfortunately shot dead on 30th January 1948. He died peacefully with the words 'Hare Rama' on his lips.

Gandhiji has thus joined the honoured list of great prophets and patriots like Jesus Christ and Abraham Lincoln who established great traditions of leadership and service and laid down their lives for the sake of their ideal. .Humanity will never forget the greatness of these noble souls.

12. The life of a great Scientist

Much of the present prosperity, comfort and happiness of he modern world is due to the great services of scientists all over the world. Many great names in the field of science can be mentioned and one can choose any one of these as a model for young students of science. One of the greatest of these scientists and benefactors of humanity was the great French Scientist Louis Pasteur (1822-1895)*He was originally a professor of Chemistry but gradually became interested in finding out the reasons why things go bad and diseases spread among the animals and the humans. He was the first man to prove that things go bad or get rotten and spoiled due to the action of the bacteria popularly called the germs. He proved that these germs are not produced by themselves but that they are carried through the air, or water, milk etc, and they grow rapidly by dividing themselves. Each part becomes a new and independent organism. Thus, a chain of the germs is created and grows. It is due to the effect of these germs that milk becomes sour, liquids like fruit juice, syrup, wine etc, becomes spoilt. Germs of disease enter the body of an animal or a human being in various ways and develope in the blood and produce violent results.

The greatness of Pasteur's work does not lie merely in finding out this abstract scientific truth. It lies in the practical help which he gave to mankind by showing how to fight against the germs and protect animals and people against these attacks. The great principles which he discovered were the following.

1) If germs producing decay or disease are destroyed (by boiling things etc.) decay or disease can be prevented. Water and milk etc. become safe from disease when it is boiled. It can be prenented from going bad if milk is boiled and then sealed to prevent germs from getting into it. This process is now called Pasteurization. The sealed and tinned foods, drinks, juices etc. can be preserved for a long time by this process.

2) A discovery even more important was the following. If the weak germs of a disease are purposely injected in the body of an animal or a person, they will produce (in reaction) antibodies in the blood. These can prevent the attack of even powerful germs later on. Pasteur proved this by giving a dose of weak germs of a desease called Anthrax to some sheep and then injecting deadly germs of this disease in their bodies after some days,' not a single sheep thus injected died, though uninjected sheeps were dying all around these.

The theory was proved even in the case of humans when weak germs of rabies could protect and cure persons against the bite of mad dogs. Thanks to this great discovery. Now we can protect ourselves against deadly diseases like Plague, Cholera, Typhoid, Diptheria, Tetanus by getting enoculated against these in advance. Thus the work of Pasteur was not merely of great scientific value; it was of great benefit to the whole of humanity by preventing deadly diseases and preserving foods for a long time.

■ ■

13. A Tiger hunt

Hunting has been an activity of necessity, profit as well as of pleasure from the beginning of human civilisation. There is something in human nature which takes delight in some kind of hunting, whatever may be the motives for such hunting. In the past, men hunted wild animals for pleasure and profit as well as for food. Now a days, such hunting of wild animals without reason is slowly being prohiabited all over the world. That is because the stock of wild animals is gradually getting smaller and smaller as the forests are being cut down and inhabited places are getting more numerous.

Still, some dangerous animals have to be shot and hunted when they turn to kill animals and human beings. Several exciting accounts of such hunts have been written by a famous English hunter Jim Corbett. This man was a great friend of the villagers of India and came to their help when wild animals became dangerous around the village. Following is a short account of such a hunt.

Corbett went out to hunt a man- eater tiger near the border of Nepal and India. The tiger had killed several animals and had even carried away women and children in open daylight from the village. A buffalo was tied to a tree and Corbett sat in the high branches of a 'tree opposite. Late in the day, the tiger jumped on the buffalo and killed it by digging his teath in the throat of the animal. Corbett fired at the tiger and expected that the tiger would fall dead. He was surprised to see the tiger jumping up and running away without showing a sign of being wounded. After some time the tiger came near the buffalo again and Carbett was able to have another shot at the beast. His surprise was still greater when he found that even after the second shot (Which seemed to hit the tiger correctly) he still ran away.

Now it was dark and Corbett had to pass the whole night in cold and discomfort on the tree. In the morning, he retuned disappointed and told the village people that he had failed to kill the tiger even shooting him twice.

He took some villagers to show them the place. To his great surprise, the people discovered not one but two tigers lying dead at some distance from each other. So Corbett learned that the tiger who came for the second time near the buffalo was not the same tiger but another one of the same size. Both the tigers were hit but did not die at once. They were so strong that they went a considerable distance before they became weak with the loss of blood and fell dead.

14. An accident which you have seen

Modern means.of transport are getting faster and faster but they do not seem to be proof against accidents. We seldom open a newspaper any morning without reading about some terrible accident happening to some motor car, railway train, a boat or steamer or an aeroplane. Minor accidents like accidents to ordinary bicycles or horse carriages are so common that they are seldom reported unless they result in a loss of human life.

The other day, I myself had and experience of such an accident and managed to escape being killed or seriously wounded just by goodluck. Some of us had formed a group to go for a holiday trip by a motor bus. We started in high spirit as the whole motor bus was engaged by our group. Some were singing chorus songs while some were talking and cutting jokes. It seemed that the noise had affected even the driver of the bus because now and then he would also turn to us and make some joking remarks. Some of us thought this to be rather dangerous and tried to warn the driver but others merely made fun of such talk.

Some two hours passed in such mirth and joy as the bus begun to climb a winding road over the mountains. The scenery was now so impressive that gradually the sounds of laughter and singing went down as we looked at the wide stretch of scenes appearing below us. suddenly, at a sharp turning, there was a loud sound of brakes being suddenly applied. We were shocked to see a small touring car approaching fast from the opposite direction and striking slantingly and dashing against our bus. The shock turned the small car completely over and its four wheels went on turning up hi the air. Our bus was not over turned but there was a loud sound of the bursting of a tyre and it suddenly fell on one side.

We all tumbled on the top of one another and I heart the sounds of cries and moans all around me. Fortunately, the doors of the bus could be opened and most of us jumped down to the help of the persons in the small car.

There we saw a terrible sight. The wind-screen and the glass windows of the car were smashed and the driver and the people inside had recieved many sharp cuts and" were covered with blood. The driver was pinned against the steering wheel and seemed to have broken some ribs. Some of the passangers in the bus had also received minor injuries and one or two had fractures of arms and legs. Fortunately, one passing-by S. T. bus stopped on the scene and carried the wounded people to a hospital near by. Others were given first-aid and rest of us were allowed to continue our journey when the usual police formailities about the report were completed and the bus was repaired. I shall never forget the scene of that accident throughout of life.

15. Visit to a place of historical importance

India is full of places of historical importance. Every State has places which are famous for some battle, some great man who was either born or who died there. Some places are famous as the capitals or places of religious importance. All these can roughly be called places of historical importance.

Last year I had an opportunity to visit Delhi, the Capital of the Republic of India. Everything about the place was strange and unfamiliar. Right at the Railway station I was surprised to see three wheeled Taxies in place of those of two and four wheels. As we rolled over the streets in a Tempo Taxi, we saw many bicycles carrying two or even three persons going on along the streets without being taken to task by any policeman.

But I was interested in historical places and not in the observation of social customs and manners. So, the next day my brother took me to see the famous Red Fort of Delhi. Three I saw the world-famous Diwan-I-Khas and Dewan-I-Aam where the Emperors used to hold their Royal Court. I was particularly interested in the Tower from which the Emperor used to show himself to the people who had gathered below. It is from this tower that the Prime Minister of India now addresses the thousands of people who gather to hear him or her on the Republic or the Independence day. On the way back we saw the Jantar-Mantar or the Astronomical Observatory, built by Raja jaising.

Next day we left by the Taj-Express to visit Agra to have a look at the world famous Taj Mahal. We had to take an old, slow moving tonga at the station and to pass through old and broken down lines of houses. All the time I went on wondering when I would see the Taj and how it would impress me. Suddenly, we came to a very High gate and were asked to get down. All we could see was a very high gate.

But when we entered through the gate, we saw a wonderful sight. There stood the Taj, in the midst of a beautiful garden. There was a canal paved with marble in the centre and the reflection of the Taj floated on it. On both sides stood tall cypress trees (Suru trees) so tall and so slender.

We approached a high plinth and climbed it to reach the main building. The square building is built of pure white marble delicately carved with verses of Holy Quran here and there. The walls rise up straight to end in a graceful, onion-shped dome in the centre. On four sides of the building rise four slenaer towars which give a perfect harmony to the building. Inside the Taj, there are the ceremonial tombs of Shahajehan and his beloved wife, Mumtaj-Mahal inside a railing, flagrant spices are kept burning here by priests in green robes. The real tombs are however underground. We went there passing over a sloping passage. At the back of the Taj, the river Jamuna flows calmly and further off, at a distance we could see the Agra Fort. It was from this place of imprisonment that poor Shaha Jehan had his last look at the Taj before his death,

Before returning to Delhi, we visited Fatepur Sikri, the town founded by Akbar some 20 miles from Agra. It is a wonderful city of palaces in red stone and marble but all the beautiful buildings are deserted. It is a city of the dead, and leaves a feeling of sadness on the mind.

In Delhi I saw later on;many othet places like the Moti Masjid, Pherozshaha Kotla, Chandani Chowk, Qutub Minar. The old ruins of Indraprastha. New Delhi, with its round Parliament house, the President's palace, Raj Ghat, the memorial to Gandhiji etc. fill the[x] mind of the visitors with wonder at the unending procession of time, which has brought such changes in the fate of this city, one of the most interesting and important cities in the world.

■　■

16. The most interesting character I (YOU) have met

The other day I went to visit my uncle who is a lawyer. With him was an old man and both of them seemed to be in a very good and merry mood. My uncle told me that he had just won a case and had got off his client, the visitor, out of the attacks of the police in the court. Their case had failed and the man was free. I asked who the man was and what he was charged with. The man himself leaned forward and introduced himself as a pickpocket! I naturally touched my pocket. The man laughed and assured me that he was not going to pick my pocket. He said, "I have just assured your uncle that I have now retired from my profession after a long and prosperous career."

I realised that he was the most interesting man I had ever met, and that I would not meet such a man again in my life. I begged him to give me some tips by which I could save my pockets from being picked by his co-workers. The man smiled and said, "We pickpockets usually select those, who are careless, Can, you imagine that many people are so foolish that they simply invite the pickpockets by their own folly! Some take out big rolls of currency notes and count them in railway trains, stations and bus stands. Then they put the notes in a big pocket book, carelessly so that a corner peeps out of their pocket. Can you blame a pickpocket if he is tempted to give it just a touch which will put the pocketbook in his hand as .the man quietly dozes ? Young men put their purses in the back pocket of their trousers and it is very easy for one of us to lift it, while standing behind him in a queue.

Ladies also are equally guilty They walk along busy roads dangling their purses and handbags just by a finger. It is easy to give just a pull and dash away in a lane before she is able to shout 'Thief. Or she puts her purse in the open plastic bag or container and walks on. One can easily lift it without her knowledge. Pens, purses, costly sun-glasses in the upper pocket of the bushcoats can be lifted just by brushing against the person and he does not even know what has happened. Even inner pockets of coats are not safe. One trick is to push against the man as if drunk and to hold on to him for support. While getting away with thanks, and patting the man on his back with one hand while the other and hand removes the walled. Pocketbooks in the right hand pocket of the trouser-pockets are lifted as the man lifts his right hand to hold the bar of train or bus to get in while a crowd pushes after him. Even the wallets kept in a vest under the bushcoat or a long coat are cut out by a man sitting near and putting his hand gently from below and cutting the pocket with a small piece of razor blade fixed to his finger-nail."

So, my young friend, if you want to save your pocket from my friends, do not do what these foolish men do. Get a pocket stitched in your underwear so that it will be on your chest to stomach and put extra money there. Always tuck your shirt inside your trousers so that no one will be able to slip his hand under it to reach beneath. A coat with the closed collar and buttoned up to the neck is safer than a coat with an oper collar held only by a button or two. Keep your loose change in the left pocket, keep your, hand on that pocket as you get in or out of trains and buses. Avoid getting into crowds just to watch some fun. It is often purposely made by the pickpockets to try their tricks. Do not go alone to the bank to withdraw big sums of money. The man standing next to you at the cash window may be a pickpocket and will follow you out of the bank to snatch your brief-case or to pick your pocket. So, my young man, never talk to strangers about the money you carry, never show your money in the open and be careful as you move in the street and as you travel. Best of all, never carry big sums in your pockets at all. Remember, prevention is better than cure. So, good luck to you." This was the most interesting character I have met.

■　■

17. The most interesting incident in my (your) life

It is difficult to choose any one particular incident in one's life, when so many incidents have their own interests. However, I particularly remember one incident in my school life which has taught me a valuable lesson.

It was the day of result of our Annual Examination of the Xth standard. We were all eager or get into the S.S.C. slass and already dreaming of our future career as doctors, engineers and lawyers. I was a a fairly good student and was sure of passing with credit. Imagine my shock when I saw my name missing from the list of successful candidates. Next day I received the result-card at home with a red line under the subject of English and with 12 marks out of 100 as my score. I ran to the teacher telling him that it was impossible as I had tried all the questions and was sure to get more than 50 marks at least. He refused to say a word and refurred me to the Head-Master.

The Head Master smiled and referred to the official mark sheet and said that my examination number 17 carried only 12 marks and so, that was the end of the matter. No answer books can be re-examined and that I had failed. He even showed the marksheet to me as s special favour.

My head was spinning like a top as I came out of the Head-Master's room. I am afraid, I must have shed a tear or two. But in a few minutes I was filled with anger. I was confident that I had answered all questions correctly and it was impossible that the total marks could come to 12 only. I went to the house of the teacher and reported the matter. The teacher smiled and as a special favour again actually showed me my answer book. Thanks to God that it was not yet sent back to the school office. He showed me the answer book No. 17 and it was not my answer book at all. No, No, I cried. This is not my answer book. I found mine at the number 11 'Look herre sir, this is my answer-book,' "The figure 17 looks like II" The teacher said; and I could not deny it. It was my fault that I had not written the number in words. But the fellow who was really 11 had also not done it. So, his answer book was taken as 17 and he got 60 marks, while my answer book was placed in the place of No. 11 and was given 12 marks.

Both the answer-books were taken to the Head Master and the handwriting of the two numbers, in all other subjects was compared. So, my marks were restored to 60 and I finally went into the S. S. C. Class. So, I always put a dash across the figure 7 and take care to see that it does not look like 11. I also remember to write the number both in figures and words to avoid such confusion. It was an escape for me and an Interesting incident to remember for all my life!

■　■

18. Scenes in an Examination Hall

An Examination Hall is a place of sharp contrasts from time to time. Before the start of the Examination, it is full of noise and excitement, as if it is a place of some popular fair. Hundreds of students arrive by rickshaws, on iifcycles, by cars and the poor on foot. It is interesting to note that many candidates are accompained by their parents or relatives, especially if-the candidates are from the countryside. These people seem to be even more anxious than the candidates themselves!

Teachers from the schools and from the coaching classes go on giving instructions to the students right up to the time of the first bell. Then the students are forced to enter the hall by themselves and to take their seats. There they sit in misery, trying to guess whether the question paper is going to be easy or difficult. There is a thrill of excitement as the Senior Supervisor arrives with the bundles of question papers and hands these over to the Junior supervisors for distribution. The students at the back try to catch a glimpse of the paper given to the candidate in front. Soon, all the papers are distributed and everyone is busy in reading these. The silence is so perfect that you can hear a pin drop.

Then the students take up their pens and prepare to write the answers which they think to be easiest. It is interesting to see how they do this. Some who have worked hard and honestly, begin to write easily and quickly. Some who are not sure are hesitating and sit chewing their pencils or pens. Some of the bolder sort try to look this way and that; in the hope that some friend may give them a few tips about the answer. Some student even tries to copy from a piece of paper he has secretly brought in the hall. He is usually detected by the Junior supervisor from his nervous manner and his guilty look. The answer book is taken away and he is taken before the Senior Supervisor for recording his statement. He is likely to lose his year. So, it is never good to try such tricks.

There is the bell after one hour and the students wonder why time passes so quickly in an Examination Hall. They begin to write even more quickly. There goes the second bell and then the warning bell, ten minutes before the time for submission of answer books. Junior supervisors run about asking students to tie up their supplements and tell them they should not leave their seats till all the answer-books are collected.

The final bell goes and the answer-books and collected. Sudents rush out in crowds feeling like birds let out from their cages! They have a hasty cup of tea, still reading their notebooks for the next paper. The scene is repeated then and so, for all the days during which the examination goes on. Only those who have gone through the process of these examinations can understand the tension under which the students have to write their papers in these Examination Halls.

■　■

19. A Railway Station

Whenever I feel bored, I always go to a Railway Station. It may seem strange, but in my case, the remedy always works. I return excited and feeling interested in all things* of life and activity once more.

The reason is clear. A Railway Station is perhaps the only place where it is impossible to feel bored. This is because it is always full of activity, hurry and excitement. Let us take a look at the station before and after the arrival of a train. See how the whole platform a filled with a crowd of struging, pushing passangers In their midst, the trolleys of the sellers of tea, sweets, newpapers etc. are calmly pushing on with their things for sale. Here is a newly married girl going to her husband's house. Her eyes are filled with tears and she can hardly keep down the sounds of her crying. Here is a group of laughing, merry students going away for a picnic. There stand some pilgrims going to visit some holy place.

Bang-bang-bang goes the bell and the excitement rises to the highest pitch. The train comes in, slowly rolling to a stop. Passengers with unreserved seats are running here and there in search of seats, shouting and cursing with anger.

There are even some fights for seats.

The upper class passenger are quietly getting in, throwing perhaps a look of amusement and contempt at the struggling and shouting crowd of poorer passenger. Friends and relatives on the platform are taking leave of the persons in the carriage and the elderly people are telling them again to take care of their tickets and money, and to write about their safe arrival as soon as they arrive at their place of stay.

Suddenly a shrill whistle blows and the guard waves a green flag. The engine gives out a loud roar and the train begins to move forward inch by inch. The noise of the people in and out of the train grows louder and falls behind, as the train gathers speed and passes out of the station.

There is a curious emptiness left in the station when a train has gone. The stream of the passengers who have arrived and of those who came to see the people off now leave the station in a slow stream. The noise and excitement now begins just outside the station as the taxies and rickshaws sound their horns and compete for the passenters going to the city. Porters run here and there with big trunks with and hold-alls on their heads and quarrel and plead for more money, however much they may be paid.

One may think that the station may be quiet now, but no, a new crowd begins to gather now for the next train and soon the station begins to hum, to shout and to roar with activity and excitement. Tell me now, is it ever possible to feel bored in such a place? So, I can confidently recommend that if you feel bord at any time, go and visit a Railway Station.

■　■

20. My favourite flower

It is rather difficult to determine which is a really best of flowers as most flowers are beautiful and attractive more or less. Yet, tastes differ as men differ. There are some who do not like the yellow *Champa* flower, While some even get a head ache when they smell the green *Champa* flower! Some find the Lily too pale and some think the *Zendu* or the sunflower too yallow and so unattractive. The Violet is too modest and the Daffodil too delicate and short-lived. The Indian *Jasmine* is liked specially by ladies while the men prefer the bolder *Mogra*.

However, if I have to cast my vote for the flower I like most, I shall declare that Rose is the king of flowers as Jasmine or Jui is the queen. A Poetess of Bengal, Toru Dutt, has written a sonnet declaring that the Lotus is the king of-flowers as it combines the red colour of the Rose and the white colour of the Lily. However, she seems to have forgotten that the Lotus has little or no fragrance though its colour and shape are graceful and attractive.

So, rather unwillingly I have to rule out the Lotus and repeat that I prefer the Rose after all.

Many poets have sung the glory of the rose. Persian poetry is particularly rich in the praise os the rose and the love of the bulbul for it. Keats sings of

"And mid May's eldest child

The coming musk rose, full of dewy wine."

Robert Burns finds a fit comaparison for beauty only in a rose and declares.....

"My Love is like a red, red rose

That blooms in the month of May. "

But enough of poets. One well have to go on repeating lines if one continues in this way. What of the common man? He will find a rose the best flower to be put in his button-hole as Pandit Jawaharlal Neharu used to do. Girls will at once say that they love to put a rose in their hair. Even little children will say that they like this flower as its petals have a sweet taste! Old men will say that a confection made from it, when it is mixed with suger (Gulkand) is a pleasant and healthful medicine.

No ceremony or function is complete until the perfume of the rose and rose water have been distributed among the guests. Thus, we can say that the Rose is the best of flowers and it holds its greatness in any form in which it might be used-fresh, dried, or even evaporated and turned into an essence as a perfume!

■ ■

Stage II (Intermediate)

21. A visit to a Bank

My brother was recently appointed to a high position in the local bank and I was pressing him to show me round his bank. So, one day he asked me to accompany him to the bank when he was free. He promised to show me all the departments of the bank.

When we came to the bank I was surprised to see a retired soldier standing guard at the door. Another one could be seen standing near the cash window where money was being paid out. My brother explained that this was to guard against any thief running out with a customer's money. First, we visited the Depositing window. You have to fill in a form entering the cash or cheques which you want to deposit in your account. The counterfoil is stamped and returned to you. The amount is credited immediately to your account if it is in cash, or on getting the payment if it is a cheque.

Then we went to the withdrawal window where you have to give the withdrawal form and Pass-book. You have to write your name, your account number and the amount which you want to withdraw (in figures and in words).

The clerk finds out from his account-book whether you have enough money in your account to enable the bank to pay you. If so, he gives you a Token or a round, coinlike metal piece with a number on it. You sit down and wait till your number is called. Then you go to the cash window, give your token and are given the money and the pass book.

Down below, in the cellar there is the safe-deposit vault which I found very interesting. A big, strong door was fixed in thick walls. You had to sign your name in a Register and give the number of your locker. The clerk checks your signature with the one he has on record. If it is correct, he comes with you inside with his key.

Inside the vault there are rows and rows of small and big lockers which are like small safes. You put in your personal key and the clerk puts in the other key which is kept in the bank. The locker can be opened only if both the keys are put in at the same time. Then he leaves you and you can put in or take out your valuables. A locker can be rented for a small amount for an year, but it saves you all the fears and worries about the theft of your ornaments or valuable document and money.

There are other departments like those dealing with granting loans, buying and selling securities, keeping Fixed deposits for a particular period, issuing Drafts on other Banks, Mail-transfer of amounts, cash credit, over-drafts etc. Most big banks in Indis are now nationalised and belong to the people. So the people should make the best use. of these without any fear of their going bankrupt (as they feared in the past). Thus my visit to the bank proved to be both interesting and instructive.

22. On strikes

Economists usually describe a stike "A weapon for collective bargaining." If one or two workers refuse to work unless the employer gives higher wages, the employer can dismiss them and can still continue his business. But if all the thousand workers in his factory refuse to work, sooner or later the employer has to make a compromise and grant at least a few of their demands. He cannot afford to keep his factory closed because that would put him to a loss of thousands every day. So, a strike is a powerful weapon in the hands of the labour today.

But this right to strike did not come to the labour easily. In the first part of the 19th centrury, workers had no right to go on strike. It was after the rise of the Trade Union movement that the right of worker to strike was admitted in certain cases. The strikes are organised by labour unions. They collect subscriptions from the workers on every pay day. When the workers go on strike, some payment is made to them from this fund. The union looks after their rights and privileges. They first approach the owners and then the government if necessary. Now a days, the government appoints some arbitrator, to listen to both the sides and gives its judgement. However, some times, the decision is not accepted by one party or the other. The owners may declare a lock-out or the workers may decide to go on a strike.

Such a strike must follow some procedure. A proper notice must be served on the owners and the grounds for the complaint must be stated. The demands must also be put forward and a definite time limit must be set for the satisfaction of these demands. A strike is then declared if the demands are not met in time.

However, all this is a matter of theory. In practice, many strikes are suddenly declared without these formalities and therefore they are called illegal. Strikes have taken place in all fields of activity, Workers in mills, factories, railways, big companies, post and even among the teachers, air-pilots and bank workers have not been uncommon.

In theory, again, certain services are declared as essential services by the government. Such as the watersupply electricity, and health services, army, navy airforce, policemen; homeguards etc. Strikes among these may be punished by imprisonment. However, strikes even among some of these department have not been unknown.

Curiously enough, strikes have never been allowed in the Communist countries like Russia and China which have a government managed by the working class. In other countries, especially in the Capitalist countries or in those concerns under private ownership, strikes are frequent.

From the national point of view, strikes result in a loss of production and of valuable man-power which remains idle. Even the workers suffer when the strikes are long drawn out. It often happens that when a strike is brought to an end, the same terms (which were formerly rejected by both side) are finally accepted. In the meanwhile, both the parties suffer a loss. To conclude, we may say that a strike is a legitimate weapon in the hands of the workers and it must not be taken away. At the same time, they must be advised to use it only rarely. The owners also must be warned that they must be fair to the workers in payment of bonus, good living conditions etc. and thus to render strikes unnecessary.

■ ■

23. Railways and their importance

The first railway was started in 1830 and ran between the two towns of Stockton and Darlington in England. It was Robert Stephenson's railway engine called *Rocket* which pulled this first train. Its speed was only 18 miles per hour but it was looked upon as wonderful. Today, we have big electric and diesel engines which can pull the trains at more than 75 miles per hour The fastest train runs in Japan at 120 miles per hours. The railways in India started with a line between Bombay and Thana in the year 1853. Then a network of railways spread over the whole country during the 19th Century.

In the western countries like England and America the railways are already becoming a back number. Passanger transport is being taken over by the quicker air travel while the movement of goods is gradually being, taken oven by the traffic of trucks on the road. But at least in Asian countries like India, the railways are still of very great importance for the movement of passengers as well as of goods. Motor traffic can never carry huge loads which the railway wagons can carry over hundreds and thousands of miles cheaply.

The real importance of the railways can be appreciated in times of emergency like war, flood and famines. It is in these critical times that the railways can carry men and materials from one corner of the country to the other quickly and far more cheaply than motor transport.

The importance of railways is not confined only to the movement of men and materials. Railways have played a very important part in the spread of civilization and economic prosperity, especially in the backward countries. Countries like Afrika, Australia, Canada, South America etc. could develop and prosper only when the railways opened these countries to the rest of the world and connected these with other centres of activity. Equally important is the part played by the railways in trade and industries. It is due to the work of the railways that shawls and apples from Kashmir are now freely available to the people of Bombay, Poona and even of Madras. Silk sarees from Banglore, Mysore and Madura are found even in the shops in North India. Railways have brought the people of different countries and different part together very closely. One has only to look at any railway compartment to find men from all parts, of all castes, creeds, communities and different languages occupying seats side by side and behaving in a friendly and familiar manner. People from far distant places like Keral and Madras think nothing of accepting jobs in Delhi, Chandigarh, Gauhatti or Dehradoon, only because they can go and return to and from these places easily by railways. So, one can say that railways have really brought about the work of National Intergration. It is in this sense also that we can say that the railway have become a part and an agent of civilized life. Indeed, they are indespensible for trade and industry.

Though railways have spread far and wide in India yet there are some parts which are still not connected with the rest of the country by the railways. Chief of these are the Konkan and part of Assam and some hilly parts of India. Another difficulty is that of a lack of co-ordination among the railway systems. We still have some lines of Broadgauge, metre gauge, Narrow gauge etc. They must all be co-ordinated and must be made up to date and efficient. Then they will help national life very greatly. Thus, the Railways have played a very important part in National development and will continue to do so, even in the future.

24. Waste not : want not

or

The importance of small savings

'Waste not, want not' is an old and popular proverb in English language. It means that if one does not waste money in unnecessary expenses, one will not be in a state of want or poverty. In other words, it suggests another English proverb which states ' Take care of the pence and the pounds will take care of themselves. ' This proverb suggests that we should start our savings even in the form of small sums. If we do that, later on, we may be able to manage even big sums.

The government of India has therefore started the ' Small Savings Scheme' for the same purpose. It encourages people to save sums even as little as 25 Paisas at a time and then go on to save larger and larger sums whenever possible. This point needs some explanation. Many people speak carelessly about small sums which are spent carelessly only because they are small. They intend to save big sums which however is seldom possible for them, even small sums saved regularly will amount to a big sum after sometimes. This is now placed within the reach of even poor people with the C.T.C. or Cummulative Time Deposit of the government and the Recurring Deposit Scheme of ordinary banks One may regularly deposit even small sums like Rs. five or ten per month and after some years get a fairly big sum of money running into hundreds of Rupees.

I The usual excuse of the people for not saving money is to say that their necessary expenses are so high that I there is no money left for any savings. This may be so, I perhaps for the labourers who have daily wages and periods of unemployment now and then. But for all others who , count on some fixed minimum income per month, savings are possible provided such people observe some system in their expenditure.

The best way is to make a monthly budget, setting aside fixed amounts for rent, food, clothing, education, medicine etc. and determine not to exceed that budget. There should be a sum regularly set aside under two heads. The first one would be that for unforeseen expenses like long sickness, festivals presents, travels etc. The second heading would be that of savings. Small sums, set aside and placed in bank under the two heads will provide a freedom from worries [i] even to a man of moderate income. He would not be forced [ii] to borrow money from others or to beg for help from others. Dickens in his novel 'David Copperfield' made one character named Micawber say some words of wise advice as 'Yearly income hundred pounds, yearly expenditure 99 pounds result happiness Yearly income 100 pounds, yearly expenditure 101 pounds-result misery.' Thus, keeping within one's income and saving regularly according to the means are the two secrets of financial stability.

Savings are not of use only to an individual. They are equally important for the well being of a nation also. Savings of the individuals placed in banks enable the country to plan schemes for the well-being and progress of the people without borrowing from foreign nations.

Postal saving banks, national saving certificates, treasury saving deposit certificates can be used for small savings. The Unit Trust is a good medium for saving and investment for' those who can save larger sums. All these means of savings bring about safety, profit and prosperity for the individual as well as for the nation.

■ ■

25. Honesty is the best policy

This is an English proverb which is often misunderstood as well as misinterpreted. The trouble lies in the word 'policy'. Some people misunderstand the word to mean that it is somthing. So, they say that one should atleast appear to be honest, even if one is not really so. But this is quite a wrong approach. The proverb mainly means that the policy or the way of our life should *always* be that of perfect honesty.

Some may object even to this simple and direct imterpretation by saying that it is not true. They point out that in various departments of life like trade, industry, advertising, law, medicine and even in social talk and behaviour people have to use dishonesty if they have to survive in this modern world of keen competition. A shopkeeper has to recommend some goods as first rate even when he knows that it is second or third rate.

At the first sight, there seems to be considerable truth in this argument, but some serious thought will show that it is a false and misleading argument. After all, the whole thing boils to a question of values in life. It depends on the person whether he chooses that. which is of a higher or better kjnd of satisfaction. Secondly, it is a question of a short term advantage or a long term advantage and reputation. One or two examples will show the truth of both these statements.

If we want to argue, for the sake of argument, we can even go to the other extreme and say that it is only by honesty that one can survive in this world of keen competition. But it is better to look to the practical side than merely to oppose one argument by another. Let us take the example of trade and even of advertising and social behaviour, the fields where honesty is not supposed to be worth following. In this connection, we have to remember the famous saying of Abraham Lincoln 'You can cheat some people for some time, you can cheat many people for some time, but you cannot cheat *all* people for *all* time.' A dishonest shopkeeper may get away with selling inferior or impure things at a good price for some time. But once his customers find out the truth, he will lose all his business. So, with advertising, a firm may sell inferior goods for some time, but will lose all buyers once they discover that the claims are false. So, in social matters also a man who is known or even suspected of being dishonest or being a liar will forfeit all respect and prestige in society. So, the truth is that though dishonesty may seem to bring some temporary profit or advantage, in the long run, it is always harmful for the man who acts in a dishonest manner.

On the other hand, it is honesty which has proved to be the best policy in national as well as international trade and finance. Many of the modern commercial transactions are carried on the assumption that the buyer is honest enough to pay the bill when it is submitted, that a cheque will be honoured when it is presented in the bank for collection. Any trader dishonest enough to refuse his obligation will be driven out of business as no one will have transactions with such a trader. Even in public life, dishonest and corrupt men are exposed some time or the other. So, we can say that both from the point of the ideal and of practical life, honesty still remains the best policy.

■　■

26. The choice of profession
or
Which profession should you follow and why ?

Every student sooner or later has the problem of choosing a profession So, it is better to think about it seriously and make up one's-mind about it. It is. usually found that this choice is influenced by the wishes of the parents. If the father is a lawyer or a doctor, he naturally wants that his son should follow his profession. No doubt, there is some advantage in such a choice because the son will have the advantage of a family tradition. However, It is wrong to force a choice on a student if he is not inclined to it. The fault also lies on the part of the student because he also does not make his choice clear to the parent. So, it is best that the student should examine the advantages of several trades and professions and choose the one for which he has a real liking. Once this choice is made, he should spend all his energies in getting the best training for it, and follow it with devotion. Success depends on perseverance and devotion. Success in any profession will bring wealth and satisfaction if it is followed with whole- hearted devotion. The choice therefore lies in individual preference and not so much in one particular profession.

The profession of accountant or an auditor or a banker is very promising and popular today. For this, the student will have to get a degree in commerce and then become a Chartered or Cost accountant or pass the Company secretary's examination. It is profession for those who have a liking for the world of commerce and finance. Next to commerce, another promising and prosperous career is that of medicine. For this, the student will have to take the Science course (Biology group) and get first class at the B. Sc. Part one examination and then spend five years more in studying Medicine and Surgery before he can begin his practice. It is a good but a rather costly and long course of study. It will suit those who have a liking for medicine and want to serve suffering humanity.

The arts course is now not so popular as it was in the past. That is because many people think that a graduate in Arts can only be a teacher which is not quite right. Of course, if he likes teaching, he can be a B.Ed, or he can go up for M.A. and become a professor if he gets a first or higher second class. If he likes law, he can get his L.L.B. degree and practice on the Civil or Criminal side and in time can rise to be a high court judge or a judge of the Supreme court. One can take up the course for a Librarian after a degree in Arts or science. Those who wish to be engineers have to take the A group for their B.Sc. part I examination and get a good class. Then they have to spend four years to be civil, mechanical, electricalor Telecommunica-tion engineer. .

Besides these courses, there are others which can be taken up immediately after passing only the S.S.C. examination.

There are diploma courses in commerce, engineering, I.T.I. courses in Radio, Motor, turning, fitting and many other technical subjects for training. Those who have finished these courses are always in demand. Other professions like Journalism, music, fine arts, theatre, film and other industries also have institutes for training the students. Thus, modern students have a very wide choice for their profession. Any one of these will lead to success if he follows it with devotion.

■   ■

27. Never venture, never have

This is a popular proverb and like most poverbs contains only a half truth. It means that one cannot have great success unless he is ready to stake or chance some thing which may succeed or may not. succeed. This is not a complete truth and the opposite view is also given in other proverbs like ' Safety first.' or ' A bird in hand is worth two in a bush.' So it is best not to take such proverbs at their face value but to judge these according to the situation and the exact circumstances in which one may be placed.

Facts in favour as well as against the proverbs may be briefly stated. First, to point out those in favour, one can say that 'fortune always favours the brave and the bold' Lives of great Generals, great men of industries or business will show that their success lay in boldly grasping an opportuty and in taking a chance. Of course, such a chance must not be taken blindly or thoughtlessly A gambler ventures his hard earned money on a throw of disc or on the fortune of cards and losees every thing. Such a venture is called blind venture. But great industrialists like Tala, Kirloskars and others knew correctly that future of industries in India was assured and ventured all their resources in their industry and achieved sucess. Merely sitting quietly without taking any chance will never lead a man anywhere to great heights of success even in services and professions. Ambitious men have;to take a chance by giving up low-paid jobs or unprofitable lines and taking up more profitable lines of work.

However one must not think that all venture and change can provide success at all times. Another proverb points out that 'A rolling stone gathers no moss' and that one can be ' a jack of all trades and a master of none.' This is the state of those who are constantly giving up the old lines of work and taking a chance of trying their fortune with every new thing, fad or fashion which comes along. Such people never suceed. Similarly, those who are rash enough to venture without proper precaution also repent. Such are those, who carry on business recklessly on the stock exchange, buying and selling shares etc. beyond their capacity. They often go bankrupt and bring misery upon themselves as well as on the members of their own family Examples of great failure in war due to uncalculated venturing can be found in history. Two of such reckless ventures which brought about defeat and failure to the whole nation and misery to millions of people are well known and recorded in history.

One of these ventures was the rash attack of Napoleon on Russia. It destroyed the 'grand army and brought about his total defeat. Later on the same foolish mistake was committed by Hitler's German Army in the World war II and brought about the collapse of Germany. The rash attack on Pearlharbour landed Japan in a disasterous war and the destruction of the whole military might of Japan.

So, we may conclude that neither a blind spirit of venture, nor an idle and cowardly state of inactivity will bring success. There must be a combination of prudence as well as the readiness to take a calculated risk if success is to be achieved. The best kind of guidance can be had from the study of men who have reached the top *in* various fields of activity in life.

One can learn from their mistakes and occasional failures and imitate only their successful ventures that is the key to success.

■ ■

28. The use and abuse of athletics and sports

It is a welcome sign in modern education that more and more attention is being paid to sports and athletics. In the past there was often a wrong idea that athletics and sports were only for those who did not care for studies and wanted to amuse themselves and others by running, jumping, wrestling and playing games like Cricket and Football. Thus, study and sports were almost kept in two watertight compartments. Now however since the last few years, our young men and women are taking more and more interest in sports and athletics without neglecting their studies.

This is really a good sign though, even now, the proportion of the students who combine both activities is not really big or satisfactory The advantages of sports and athletics must be emphasized and liking for these must be cultivated right from the school days. It is wrong to think that athletics and sports develop only the body. They provide valuable mental and moral training also. They make the body healthy and strong and teach self control, courage and resourcefulness. Modern team events in athletics and team games like Cricket, Hockey, Football, Basketball develop team spirit, tolerance and co-operation. On the sports ground, all distinctions of caste, creed, nationality, status (of the rich and the poor) are all forgotten. Thus, sports and athletics provide valuable lesson in liberty, equality and fraternity (brotherhood). They provide healthy recreation and entertainment for the body as well as to the mind. They refresh the mind and encourage mental efforts and achievements.

However, we must not be blind to the other side of the picture also. The old prejudice against athletics and sports was due to the excess and the extreme to whkii these activities were taken by some sportsmen. An excess even in some thing good will result in some thing bad; so also with athletics and sports. Weight-lifting beyond one's capacity etc will affect the heart. That is the cause why some athletics have died untimely. Similarly, too much interest in events and tournaments will prevent a student from devoting his attention to the studies. Flatterers and admirers of such sportsmen are the really guilty parties who make such sportsmen lose their sense of balance and proportion.

There is also a temptation of making such activities a kind of profession by accepting money for these. Once a student gets the taste of such professional engagements, he loses his interest in all academic achievements. So, we some times see a promising college student with an undue liking for sports becoming an ordinary drill master, games master or P.T. director. Unfortunately, these positions in India are never wellpaid and such men have to live a life of poverty and frustration.

So we may conclude that sports and athletics have a very important part to play in education as well as in social life later on. However, one must guard against an excess in these activities. They should be given their proper place in activities of one's life.

29. Horrors of modern war

One can say that horrors have existed in war even from ancient times. Even when men fought only with bows and arrows or with sticks and swords, horrible wounds were inflicted on the opponents no doubt. Yet, these wars were looked upon as heroic and noble.

All this is now changed mainly because machines are used for fighting in the place of the simple weapons of war used in hand to hand fighting as in the past. The mechanical warfare can produce wounds far more horrible than those ever imagined in the past. Old fighting and battles had their own rules of fair play. An unarmed soldier or a civilian was seldom struck down. Fighting was confined only to the professional soldiers. They fought the wars while the common people carried on their activities peacefully around. Modern wars have changed all these conditions. They have taken away all romance and personal heroism from war. There is nothing heroic in simply pulling the trigger of a machinegun and cutting down any soldiers or innocent man, woman or child that comes within its range. Even more horrible is the action of bombing cities from the air. Napalm bombs and bombs setting fire to houses can produce horrible burning wounds bringing painful death to the innocent men, women and children in cities. A bomb dropped from the air does not spare an innocent child or even the patients lying helplessly in hospitals.

But the horror of war is not confined only to guns and cannons, bombs and rockets. Far more dangerous and horrible means of destruction are now ready in the hands of scientifically advanced nations. In 1945, America dropped two atom bombs on the Japanese cities of Hiroshima and Nagasaki. They killed about 80,000 persons at once and thousands more died slowly and horribly in the years which followed. Atom and hydrogen bombs, far more powerful than the first atombombs of 1945, are now ready in hands of advanced nations like America, England, France, Russia and China. It is calculated that a few dozens of such atom bombs might wipe out the whole population of thickly populated countries like England and Japan. Intercontinental rockets or missiles can now be fired across hundreds and thousands of miles with accuracy merely by pushing a button. So, the, next world war is likely to be called 'the push button war'. A Russian scientist may push a button and his rockets with atomic war heads may destroy a huge city like New York. An American or English scientist may do the same with Moscow or Leningrad.

Happily enough, even more horrible means of distruction are- by common consent of nations- now prohibited. These are the methods of germ war-far and the use of nerve gas. Deadly germs of diseases like plague, cholera, Typhoid, meningites may be dropped over the water supply of a city and kill thousands. Bombs containing deadly gases might burn out the lungs of men or paralyse thousands.

Such are the horrors of war those which have actually taken place and those which can take place in the future. It is a happy sign that the people of the powerful nations have become concious of the horrors and the great dangers which they hold for the whole humanity. It is sure that once a third worldwar starts, one side or the other will make use of one or the other of scientific means of destruction. The other side will follow suit in return. As a result, there is a danger that the whole humanity may be wiped out from the surface of the earth as great men like Burtrand Russell have feared. So, the future of man-kind lies in banishing all great wars and the horrors of such wars.

30. Conquest of the air

From ancient times, man has always dreamed of conquering the air and flying through it. In those times, it was not actually practical for him to do so. So he satisfied himself by doing so in imagination and description in poetry. So we have the Greek story of Icarus who flew in the air by attaching wings to his sholders. In *Ramayana,* we have description of *Pushpak* air-ship in which Ram and Seeta returned from Lanka to Ayodhya. In *Mahabharat,* we have a more realistic description of the airship of Shalva from which he bombed Dwaraka.

However, the first practical experiments of flying were made in 18th century in France by Montgolfier brothers. They made a big balloon and attached to it pan of burning coal. The heated air then carried the balloon in the air. Then in early part of the 19th century, came the round and cigar (cylinder) shaped airships filled with tanks of hydrogen. They did not require any fire under them. They carried men to the exact place they liked because the airships could be guided by a rudder. It could go up by throwing down bags of sand and could come down by letting out the hydrogen gas from a tank or two. Such big airship continued even in the 20th century with the German Zeppelines (used in the first world war) But they were given up because hydrogen could easily catch fire and several air ships like R 30 were burnt out killing many people on the board. Such air ships will never be used in future. These are called ' lighter than the air' ships.

A better and more safe aeroplane was discovered by 1905 by two American brothers Wilbur and Orville Wright. They used one petrol engine to give speed to the airoplane with two wings until it left the ground and flew in the air. This was the real begining of the age of the conquest of the air. The aeroplane developed very repidly. Soon, there were more and more powerful petrol engines and airplanes with several such engines could fly higher, faster and for longer distances. These were called 'petrol-driven aeroplanes with propellers.' The American, Charles Lindburg crossed the Atlantic ocean in a single engine aeroplane. A woman named Amy Johnson flew nonstop from England to Australia alone.

The next important developement in the construction of the aeroplanes came with the invention of the *Jet engine* during the second world war. It simiplified the construction and did away with the need of heavy and unsafe petrol engines with pistons. Such powerful series of Jet engines have made possible huge Boeing 707 aeroplanes which can, carry hundreds of passangers and can fly round the world without a stop!

But the most wonderful step in the conquest of the air and the space even above the air (on the earth) is provided by the Rockets or Spaceships. It is in such a rocket that Armstrong and Collins travelled from the earth to the moon and back.

However, The dangers of bombing from the air, hi-jacking the aeroplanes, crashing etc. have been the serious disadvantages of such conquest also. On the whole, how ever, man's conquest of the air is a wonderful achievement.

■ ■

31. Pleasures of reading

There are many pleasurers which a man can enjoy in his life but most of them have their limitations. Pleasures like sport and play can be enjoyed only in childhood and early youth. Pleasures of eating are also limited by physical capacity and power of digestion. They lose their appeal in sickness and in extereme old age. The same can be said about several other pleasures which depend on youth and physical strength. The pleasure of reading is only the pleasure which can be enjoyed right from childhood down to the last days of a man's life.

Reading requires neither health nor physical strength. It does not require any considerable expense and can be enjoyed at any time of the day and the night, in any place, whether in a crowd or when alone. It is the purest of pleasures and the most lasting and permanant. Now-a-days books with very large type are avalable to those with weak eyesight and even the blind can get the pleasure of reading by using books printed in the Braille type. They can use their fingers which pass over the page and can read. The latest development is that of reading-machines by which one can read a book which is projected on a screen page by page and the talking books which one can hear without making any jise of eyes or spending any'energy in turning the pages while reading.

Reading has several uses which are often looked upon as more important than pleasure. They are information, education, communication, propaganda etc. However, the pleasure which reading can give should not be looked upon as less important than these practical uses. However, it is true that the taste for such a pleasure has to be cultivated and does not come naturally as the taste for food comes naturally to the people. The pleasure of reading is greatest reward of a cultivated and cultured mind. The best way in which this pleasure can be cultivated is by developing a liking for reading right from the school days. Once a person gets this liking, he has a priceless treasure of the whole world of literature open before him. The wealth of this treasure is so vast that not one but several lives, all spent in reading will not be able to exhaust it.

However, one must remember that there are pleasure, and pleasures. This means that some pleasures are low and mean while some are good; some better and a few the best. In other words, true pleasure of reading comes from reading the best and the greatest books.

No doubt, some people may get some kind of pleasure from reading low and worthless kinds of books like crime and common detective stories and novels. But it is not the highest kind of pleasure. One reads such a book and throws it away. One forgets a temporary pleasure and seeks the next. It becomes almost a vice or a craze for an intoxicating drug without which one feels uneasy and unhappy. Real pleasure of reading never turns into such a vice. It is the wholesome pleasure which makes the reader happier, better, noble. Of course, one can get most pleasure from the kinds of books one really likes-poetry, drama, novel, short story, essay, history etc. In each kind, one should select the best and the highest books and get the best, highest and most lasting pleasure which human life can give to a person.

■　■

32. On advertisements

Sixty four arts were mentioned in ancient indian literature. A great modern Marathi writer named Mr. N. C. Kelkar called the art of advertisement the sixty-fifth art in human life. This may appear to be rather an exaggeration, but it has an element of truth in it, atleast in the modern times.

We do not come across advertisement on a large scale in old literature or even in the newspapers and magazines till the 19th centurey. Till then, any kind of advertisement was carried out by the word of mouth by friends and servants, in the form of plackards or speeches etc. The real and excessive developement of advertisement dates from the middle of the 19th century, with the growth and spread of cheap newspapers and magazines. Industrial development, invention of better machins, making mass production possible, created huge stocks of goods of all variety. How were they to be sold? The only way of doing this was by trying to persuade as many people as possible to purchase these things. This could be done only by the use of advertisements.

Older advertisements in the later part of the 19th century were more or less only a description of the goods, statement of the price and the place where it could be purchased. It ended by a request to the reader to purchase that product.

However in modern times, advertisements have become really a fine art and a very complex one. Advertising itself has become a huge business requiring a good knowledge of human psychology besides the usual kinds of information required for advertising a product.

The modern advertiser proceeds by making use of every device provided by modern science to catch the attention of the people and to persuade them to buy the product. All means for catching the attention while pleasing and amusing the public are used by advertisers. Fine pictures are painted by artists, attractive posters and huge hoardings are placed by the side of the roads to catch the attention of people even when they are travelling. Advertisements with attractive photographs, pictures etc. are common enough in newspapers and magazines. But the latest devices taken over by the advertisers are the radio, the cinema and the television.

Everybody must have seen the short advertisements on the cinema screen showing an interesting scene of home life dealing with children, husbands and wives, parents and grandparents. After telling some interesting story or incident, the advertiser cleverly shows his product and impresses on the mind of the spectator that it is in his interest to use that product. The radio makes use of fine music, vocal as well as instrumental, speech which is attractive or humorous in order to persuade the hearer to buy that product. Advertisers on the radio and the television spend thousands and millions to present attractive programmes, stars and singers before the public so that their product may become linked in the public memory with the programme.

It is often objected that such advertising is now becoming rather a nuisance. Hoardings spoil the beauty of the countryside, advertisement on the cinema screen, the radio and the television spoil the pleasure of seeing and listening to more interesting items. The cost of advertising makes the products dearer. Yet, with all these objections, advertisements continue and will continue even in future because they have become an inseperable part of our age.

■ ■

33. "Neither a borrower nor a lender be"

This line of advice comes from the famous speech of advice given by a character named Polonius in Shakspear's play 'Hamlet'. Polonius gives a long list of practical and useful instructions to his son Laertes, who is going to France for his education. Before discussing this particular item of instruction, it is necessary to note that Shakespeare, (the writer) himself has made these instructions to reflect the character of Polonius. He is a talkative, worldly- minded old man who thinks himself to be very wise. So, his instruction appears to be worldly wise but not upto the highest standards of conduct. In other words, these words of advice are to be taken with a reservation and must not be blindly followed under all circumstances.

For ordinary purposes, the advice is largely true Polonius explains his statement by saying-

"Neither a borrower nor a lender be
For the loan oft loses itself and the friend
And borrowing dulls the edge of husbandry. "

Any one can remember an example some time in his life, how he had lent some money to his friend and how that friend never returned that money. When the lender insists on repayment, there is often a quarrel and the friendship is at an end. Secondly, a habit of borrowing takes away the desire to work hard. 'Dulls the edge of husbandry' means that the borrower losses his taste and liking for hard work (if he can get money more easily by borrowing from some one else.) So, for ordinary purpose, it is best to see that one does not borrow from others and does not also lend to others. If you once borrow for yourself, you cannot refuse to lend to others. So, it is best to make it clear to all that you will neither borrow nor lend. Thus you can set up a standard for living your life facing any difficulty which may occur.

However, it is easier to give such an advice than to observe it. Men of the middle class and the poorer class often feel obliged to borrow money at the end of the month and so, they have to lend it to others who may be in similiar difficulties. One cannot refuse help to a dear friend when the need is real. Otherwise, it would be an example of heartless conduct. However, excepting the case of real necessity, it is better not to lend money. One should not borrow unless it is unavoidable.

This advice is true in private life only. It breaks down completely in the fields of modern commerce and finance. Every trader has to borrow money from the bank for his business, expansion, execution of orders etc. He can never avoid borrowing money or asking for over-draft, cash credit etc. In the same way, he has to lend money also. Placing money in the bank is as good as lending it to the bank which promises repayment. Supplying goods on credit to customers is also a form of lending. So are the forms of hire purchase, selling on instalment basis, etc. All these kinds can never be avoided in modern business. Of course, borrowing and lending, even in business must be kept within one's limit and capacity. Thus, the statement is largely true in personal life but not at all true in fields of commerce and finance of today.

■ ■

34. On newspapers

Newspapers have become a necessity of modern life. So, we usually take these for granted and think that they must have been there for all times. But that is not so. The newspapers came very late in the form in which we know these. There were small news-sheets (like handbills) in 16th and 17th centuries in England. But they were not regular or daily newspapers in the modern sense. In the 18th century, came the Periodicals published twice or thrice per week, but they were literary in their form rather than being informative like the modern newspapers.

Newspapers chiefly devoted to publishing the latest news from various parts of the country, began to appear in the 19th century and were called the Gazettes. They were however, very limited in their information and news because it was difficult to bring the latest news from distant places to the office of the newspapers. Newspapers began to be more varied and informative as the railways and steamers brought regular news and the postal system sent letters quickly and regularly. It was the invention of the telegraph, that first made a world-wide coverage of news possible. Then came the inventions of the telephone, the ocean cables and the wireless telegraph and radio. With these inventions the news papers were able to bring the latest news of all the world to the door step of the reader within a few hours of their happening.

But newspapers do not carry news only. Modern newspapers aim at providing light interesting reading to every person of whatever taste with reading material which is up to date. The father of the family interested in politics gets the latest political and financial news. Younger members of the family find interesting items of sport or entertainment or even of education, if they want it. The ladies in the family find useful articles on home life and domestic problems. Even little children find comics and songs and stories to their liking.

But the newspapers are not only for entertainment or information. They have been called the 'Fourth estate' or the fourth important force in a country besides the army, the navy and air force. It is well known that most newspapers belong to one political party or the other, while a few belong to no party but put forward independant views. Whatever be the political views, the newspapers are powerful force in the country. They can control the views and votes of thousands of people. This is seen especially at the time of the elections.

There are a few example of undesirable activities of 'Yellow Journalism" or newspapers being used for sensational news and articles throwing contempt on the opponents, to screw out money from them. Some take bribes and write in favour of those who pay them. Some flatter the rich or the ruling party and get advertisements and money.

But on the whole, the majority of newspapers observe the code of right conduct and are great force in national life. They form the cheapest and the most useful instrument of mass education and information. So, they must be supported and encouraged. Newspapers with a big circulation can support themselves but the smaller and local newspapers must be supported and encouraged by the Government as they also play an important part in national life.

35. ' Safety first'

This is slogan or loud expression which has its right as well as wrong applications. It is the slogan of the First Aid organization and of the Road Traffic organizations. It is well known that most of the accidents on the road are due to the rashness of the drivers. They try to dash forward taking a chance that the road might be clear, when it is not clear, there is a collision and smash up. It is better to be late by five minutes in this world than to go fifty years too early in the next world!

But safety is to be observed not only in traffic but also in many other occasions in everyday life. A few examples will be sufficient to prove this. In finance and investment, it is dangerous and unsafe to put one's money in a venture which promises a very high rate of interest. Higher the rate of interest, less is the safety. This is a golden rule in finance. Similarly, It is dangerous to try remedies suggested by unqualified persons simply because they have done good to somebody. It is equally unsafe to build a house with cheap but doubtful materials depending on luck. Such a building may collapse and destroy property as well as life. So, proper care of safety must be taken in giving medicines to children and the sick people. There are cases in which mothers have given medicine in darkness mistaking a poisonous drug for a good drug and the child has died. So, for safety, poisonous drugs should never be kept near normal drugs.

Safety must be the first care in using the advanced types of home appliances like fans, pressure cookers, geysers, electric ovens, electric irons etc. Even a simple action like changing an electric lamp bulb has brought about deaths when the person carelessly touches the points of electric contact. Even pedestrains (persons walking along the road) get cought in accidents when they try to cross a road without looking at the coming traffic. Cyclists are often in trouble as they pass by carriages or try to catch a passing truck and hang on its end. Passengers in railway trains and buses try to get on or off vehicles while they are in motion and meet with accidents. Some young men think it to be fun to stand on the footboards of trains and suffer the penalty when they fall off or dash against a pole along the railway track. Thus, it is best to put the consideration of 'Safety first' in such matters rather than acting hastily and repenting afterwards.

However, this principle must not be taken to be an unexceptional truth for all time. There are occasions in life when considerations of personal safety must be kept aside for the sake of duty. If there is a war, one must not say 'Safety first' and keep away. It is the duty of every young man to come forward to help the couiury in any way he can, even at the cost of comfort, convenience and if necessary at the cost of his life also. Similarly, in times of Fire, floods, Death, family disasters, one must keep the considerations of safety aside and must do one's duty. To keep away for safety would be looked upon as cowardly on such occosions.

So, to conclude, we may say that in the matters of everyday life and activity, ' safety first' makes a very useful rule of our conduct. It will save us from many dangers and troubles. However, in times of national emergency and family troubles and dangers, it has to be set aside for brighsr considerations of duty and honour.

■ ■

36. Are we happier than our forefathers?

The young people of today are accustomed to modern conveniences like the railways, motor cars, the radio, the cinema. Sometimes they openly express their wonder how the people of older times could live without these conveniences. They shudder when they think of the old, dim oil lamps, the insanitary conditions of W. C.s without the modern flush-system, the lonely evenings without entertainment like cinemas etc. From this, they make a general statement that afterall, they are much happier than the people of the past times. They can support their statements, no doubt, with other arguments also. Better remedies for diseases, a greater variety of food etc. have made our life safer and more comfortable.

However, the question given above cannot be so easily answered. We may grant that we have more physical comfort than the people of the past, but that is not so in mental conditions. Modern life is full of a cut-throat competition filled with mental strain and worry. The fight is harder among individuals and the jealousy between nations frequently brings about wars in which thousands and millions of lives are dost. Compared with this, the older battles and wars affected only the professional soldiers. Even the doctors confess that there are for more cases of nervous breakedowns and even of insanity, cases of high blood pressures, of heart diseases, paralysis, polio and Cancer than there were at any time in the past. Then how can we say that we are really happier than our ancestors ? Mere increase in material comfort is not the same as an increase in happiness. Happiness is something better and brighter than mere comfort or pleasure.

Most of our ancestors lived in villages and knew nothing of the comforts and conveniences mentioned above. They cultivated their fields and spent their evenings in quiet talk with thek friends. They went to bed early at night and did not miss the bright lamps which we have today. They did not feel the need of many::;, of the fine things which we look upon as necessary for our life. They were contented with what they had, and after all, contentment is true happiness.

Ancient religious teachers taught the virtue of contentment and simplicity of life as leading to real happiness. Socrates, Diogenes, Buddha, Gandhiji all taught that the man who could keep his persct-al desires and needs as few as possible had the greatest chance of being happy.

We seem to have forgotten this teaching. No man seems to be content with his lot today. Every one wants a big salary, a fine flat or house, a car, a 'refrigerator etc. and feels unhappy if he cannot afford these things. Naturally, the people who can have such things are comparatively few. The vast number of others are therefore left unsatisfied, burning their hearts with envy, jealousy and bitterness. Thus, they lose whatever happiness they could have in their own conditions. It is only in the respect of health, medicine and control of pain that we can really say that we are better off than our forefathers. Lastly, we must realise that pleasure is not happiness. It lies in the state of mind. It is only in the inner happiness of the spirit, a sense of contenment and satisfaction and mental peace that we can get real happiness. From this point, we do not seem to be happier than our forefathers.

37. Students and politics

Whether students should take part in politics or keep out has been a hotly debated question since the struggle for independence. Strangely enough, this question has not been definitely settled one way or the other, even today. That is because the problem is a complex one and has various terms and conditions in it. Basically, the politics is a science of the ways and methods of government. It is one of the subjects of study for higher classes in a University and many students study this subject along with economics. However, when we talk of students and politics, we do not mean only the study of this branch of knowledge in theory. What we mean is whether students should *actively participate* in practical politics like making speaches, taking part in political processions, canvassing for candidates of a particular political pary, taking part in 'Morchas, Hartals, Gheraos'.

The temptation for entering into these activities is placed by the political parties before the students because such parties always stand in need of enthusiastic supporters and workers like the students. More over, the students are so idealistic that they usually work without any payments which is exactly what many leaders want and welcome. That is why we find that every political party tries to attract students and to make them work for its programmes. For a time, she students also get a feeling that they are doing some very important national work and feel a sense of satisfaction and fulfilment in it.

In principle, it can be said that there is nothing wrong if

students take interest in politics and even take their share in the work of the party which they prefer. As the citizens of a democratic country like India, this is their birth-right. It was not so when the British ruled over India and issued strict circulars and orders forbidding students from taking any part in politics. However, in their enthusiasm, students must not forget a few plain but vital facts as their future depends on these.

For this purpose, we have to divide students in to two unequal groups. There is very small group of students who decide to enter politics right from their school and college days. For them, there is no question. They must train themselves for a political career from their student days. But a large majority of students have no such ambition. They intend to follow some trade, profession or service. Will it be any advantage for them to take part in active politics which will necessarily affect their studies? The answer is clearly in the negative. Of course, they can watch, feel interested in politics and should study all schools and parties of politics. But they should also remember that it requires many years of deep study in active experience before one can be a politician. Their first duty is to study and make themselves fit for thejc career for which they came to the school or the college. .They should guard themselves against being exploited by political parties which push them first and foremost to suffer Lathi-charges, tear gas, firing and imprisonment but run away with the prize of profitable positions of leadership when the occasion arises. Then these students are completely neglected and left to their own fate and often spend their life in some minor job or unemployment, repenting for their folly. So, it is best for students to study and observe politics in their student days instead of entering the rough political life unless they want to make politics itself their lifelong career.

38. The language problem in India

The language problem has assumed a serious and threatening form in India since independence. Strangely enough, similar heat or bitterness about languages was not found in the country during the British rule. The problem has become very complicated because there are three different and distinct schools of thought and each one insists that its own policy should be accepted throughout the country. It is necessary to understand something about each of these views before coming to any conclusion about this problem. These three views are 1) Hindi should be the language of all government and interprovincial communication and the medium of instruction. 2) The regional languages only should be used for administration of each state and the medium of instruction. English should be used as the means of interproivincial communication. 3) English as before should be used for administration, interprovincial communication and even as the medium of instruction for higher classes, and colleges.

Each of the three views has found strong supporters and the support often turns to an attack on the policies of the opposing group. The supporters of Hindi take their stand on the fact that Hindi is now declared to be the National language of India. They argue that regional languages will break up the unity of the country. They hold that Hindi will take and can take the place of English, even in higher and technical field through Hindi translations of standard English books. They point out that Hindi is known all over the north and the central part of India and can be learnt and understood even in the south in a short time.

Those who argue in favour of English sa^ that English is a world-language and hot the monopoly of England only. It is the richest of all western language because it contains the treasures of all other languages (in translations.) By keeping out English, our country will be cut-off from the rest of the civilized and prograssive world. By adopting English, there will be no unfair advantage given to people of any regional language, even Hindi cannot be free from such unfair advantage to the native speakers. It will unify the people of the whole country and make interstate relationship easy. It is nothing new but only carrying on the established policy and will not require any whole-scale change-over as in other policies. Simpler and better methods of teaching English, right from primary schools can easily bring knowledge of English even to the uneducated within a few years.

Those who support regional languages argue that both Hindi and English are equally unfamiliar to the people at large. The use of regional language is the only natural and logical activity for every state in 'India. It is the principle on which linguistic states were formed in India and we must not go back upon it. All the administrative and commercial transactions within the state can be carried out in regional languages. Interprovincial communication can be either in English or Hindi, according to the choice of each state by free preference.

These three views have produced much bitterness and even violence and blood-shed. The advocates of English are now in a background but the claims of Hindi and regional languages are still hotly debated. In the matters of states, regional languages are naturally important and an option for' Hindi or English should be given to the states for other purposes, of interprovincial communication. This will be the best solution of the present language problem.

39. Village Reconstruction and Uplift
Or
Cummunity projects

'Vinoba Bhave rightly criticised the early five year plans' by saying that they had neglected the poor villagers and were aimed at making cities and industries rich and better. Later five year plans have tried to remedy this unbalanced state by giving more attention to village uplift and reconstruction. Yet, even now, the situation in the villagers is not quite satisfactory.

During the British regime, the villages were purposely neglected and the farmers kept in a low position so that they should not indulge in any political activity. It was Gandhiji, who started the 'Back to the villages movement' advising young men to go to the villages-and help in their reconstruction. However, not much could be done be done as the energy of the whole nation was devoted to the struggle for freedom.

The start of the community project scheme was made on second October, 1952. An elaborate scheme of planned economy and social service was formulated. 50 projects were taken up and divided into 75 developement blocks, each under a regional development officer. The finance for the project was to be contributed by the government and the labour by the people. Technical co-operation by the authorities of T.V.A. project in America was forthcoming. Each community project covered 300 villages. Each block covers 100 villages. There are usually three blocks in each project. A project roughly covers 500 sq. miles and affects 600-700 thousand people. Aim of the community project is to raise the cultivated area to 1,50,000 Acres and the whole scheme is to affect 16 million people when the project is completed. The total expenses are estimated at

40 crores out of which 4 crores are contributed by America. This has led to some criticism about American influence but the aid is only 1/10, without any political conditions. The programme of the project aims at the following :- building roads and bridges, providing electricity for light and power; . providing schools, hospitals and community centres for each village; providing better seeds, fertilizers, digging wells, bunding, clearing, terracing, using tractors for ploughing, setting up co-operative societies for the distribution of seeds, tiles, crude oi| etc; Setting up co-operative Banks to provide credit for puchasing engines, tractors, implements. Setting up Cultural activities like folk songs, folk dances, dramas, Social reform, discouraging drinking, early marriages, untouchability and other harmful customs etc.

In short, village reconstruction is the aim to be achieved through the community Projects. These are not as charity or gifts. They are a co-operative effort by which the villagers are to be taught to make their lives better. In this effort the Government will contribute finance and technical personnel and know-how. The people of the villages are to contribute man power and to become gradually self-sufficient. If this project is successful, then within a generation, the Indian villages will change beyond recognition. They will be as advanced and as comfortable as the cities. Then the craze for leaving villages for the luxuries and glamour of the cities will end. The people in the villages will be satisfied with living in their villges. Then in the future, the difference between the cities and the village will be wiped out as it is in England and America.

40. On Nationalism

Nationalism is generally understood as the love of the one's country and a pride in it's greatness. In its purest form it is a noble sentiment natural to every man. Sir Walter Scott has well asked—

"Breathes there a man with a souls so dead ?
who never to himself has said
This is my own, my native land"?....

However, in its impure and violent form the same sentiment may produce untold harm and wholesale death and destruction for millions of people. So, This sentiment must be carefully considered and followed with discrimination.

In its present form, this feeling is comparatively recent in the west. Till the Renaissance, Christian nations were in a group and the separate consciousness" of each natio*n was not roused to the present extent. After Renaissance came the break up of the Christian Church as well as of the political groups and each nation began to be conscious of its own special rights, privileges and culture. With the discovery of new countries in the East and the West, Nationalism began to turn into Imperialism as each country began to grab the newly discovered countries to make itself great and powerful. England, France, Spain, Portugal, Holland etc. grabbed these lands and set up their own Empries. Systematic efforts began to be made to make each country conscious of the heritage of such empires. Every country began to teach the children that it was the best and its culture alone was the best in the world.

In this situation a clash of interests was inevitable. It brought about disastrous wars between two nation. These wars began as early as the 16th century. They have continued till today through the Napoleonic wars, the Franco-Purssian war. The first world war and the second world war. They rose from the insistence of each nation that it alone was great and that it must have power, wealth and advantages of trade, commerce, government over the native people of the countries that it may conquer. Industrieal and scientific advance did not lesson this conflict but on the other hand intensified it. It drew in even the nations like America which did not want colonial empires.

20 the century saw the intense intolerance of such Nationalism. The fascists and the Nazis in Italy and Germany openly declared that they were determined to create great empires for their nations even at the cost of attacking the other nations because they alone were great nations. The two great world wars were the result.

It is therefore that the great thinkers like Dean Inge, Bertrand Russell, Gandhi]! and Nehru have attacked this aggressive kind of Nationalism and have advised the people to develop Internationalism and to look upon the whole world as a unit. Vinoba has given the slogan *Jai Jagat* to show that each man should look upon himself as a citizen of the world, and not of a narrow state. Wendell Wilkie, H. G. Wells and Bertrand Russell have put forward a serious proposal for a World Parliament and a World Government with an International army, navy and airforce. But the proposal has not been found to be practical till now.

Nationalism in its pure form is a great creative force and has brought about the rise of free India and the Asian and African countries. But if it is misused to serve narrow national interests at the cost of others, it can be very dangerous as has been seen in the unjust policies of Germany, Italy, South Africa, Rhodesia and recently of Uganda. Uganda has driven off all Asians so that the natives of Uganda alone will have the unchallenged scope for all profitable occupations. Persecution of the black people by the minority of whites in South Africa is another examples of bad Nationalism.

41. Pen is mightier than the Sword

This is one of the epigram -like statements which is constantly being quoted like proverb. In the statement, the pen stands as a symbol or a sign of the mind, the written words while the sword is a symbol of military power. So in simple words, the statement means that laws, literature or intellectual power are stronger in the end than mere brute force.

At the first sight, the statement does not appear to be literally true. One may very well object by saying that a man with a sword in his hand will be able to kill even ten men holding pens in their hands- they may be poets, writers, novelists etc. But the statement must not be taken so literary. What the writer wants to say is as follows; kings and generals might have very great power of the sword and may conquer various countries with their swords. But their money, their reputation and influence live only for a short time, at the most while they live. After their deaths, they are either forgotten or even looked 'upon as cruel and hateful. Conquerors like Changizkhan, Taimur Lung, Mohmed of Gazni, Nadirshah and even men like Alexandar and Napoleon are example of men commanding great military power and great success with their sword. But how long did their empires last? For a very short period. Their swords were without any power to oppose the passing of time. On the other hand, great poets like Homer, Kalidas, Shakespeare Milton, Tulsidas, Surdas etc. have created works which have lived for hundreds and hundreds of years. They are mighty that they can go on living till the end of time. But the names of the kings who ruled when these writers lived have already been forgotten. This is the real proof of the statement that the pen is mightier or stronger than the sword.

The statement can also be taken in another sense. Here

the word 'mighty' can be taken to stand for spiritual, moral strength. The sword may force the people to act in a particular manner by compulsion. But as soon as the power of that sword is gone, the people will give up the ways they were forced to adopt. But if the pen (meaning great and eloquent writers, philosophers, and teachers) says the same things, their influence will last far longer. Examples of reforms like prohibition enforced by law can illustrate this fact. More people have been persuaded not to drink liquor by the effect of great works of art like the Marathi play 'Ekach Pyala' or the novel 'Dram-shop' by the French novelist Zola or the English novel ' Danesbury-House' by Mrs. Henry Wood than by any law of prohibition. Even if tomorrow a law against smoking is passed, it will be broken like prohibition. However, when great scientists and doctors prove completely that smoking necessarily leads to Cancer of the lungs, these writings will be far more effective.

However, for practical purposes, a nation requires men who can use the sword as well as those who can use the pen. When it comes to actual survival, it is the sword which has to protect the pen or the men who make use of pen and the works which they produce. So, both the pen and the sword are equally necessary for a nation ana* it is idle to run down one at the expense of the other.

■ ■

42. Work is worship

This is famous principle which was eloquently preached by Carlyle, a great writer of the 19th century in England. In India the same principle was poetically expressed by various poets like Rabindranath Tagore, Ramdas, Tukaram and others. They all point out that it is wrong to take a narrow view of worship as only some prayers offered to God in a temple. The real worship of God lies in work which is done for the good of others. Such work is appreciated by God as worship.

This has been explained by Jesus Christ in the Bible itself. Christ openly said to his disciples that whenever they helped some poor, sick or helpless persons, their good action would be taken as worship by him. Gautam Buddha also preached kindness towards all, including the animals. This would be taken as part of worship itself.

However, work is not restricted only to showing kindness or helping others. Such work can be taken as a religious duty and so it is easy to look upon it as a form of worship. But Carlyle, Tagore and Ramdas and Tukaram go one step farther. They declared that any honest, sincere and- hard work, done even as a matter of duty has the same importance and value as that of the worship of God. Tagore even bluntly asks the worshipper in the Dark temple to go out and work hard in fields or on the road, side by side with the labourers. When Shivaji wanted to leave his work of liberating the country and wanted to live a life of worship and devotion, the saint Ramdas gave him a similar advice, so did another saint Tukaram. They both pointed out that it was not necessary for Shivaji to leave his work, spend his time in the ceremonies of worshipping God. He could serve God better by doing his duties as a king by liberating his country and giving the people peace, justice and prosperity. A learned man and judge named Ramshastri Prabhune gave similar advice to the Peshwa, Madhawrao, whom he found spending too much time in ceremonies of worship!

The same argument may be extended to intellectual work. We have many great scientists like Pasteur, Lister, Einstein, Edison and others who spent the whole of their life in working in their laboratories or study rooms. Many of these were not known to take part in the orthobox prayers and services of religion as some other very religious people often did. In fact, now it has become almost a fashion to accuse the scientists of being men without religion. But a little thought will show that if they do work which is useful for humanity, that work is as good as any worship in a temple or a church. Even a farmer producing corn, a soldier protecting his country at the risk of Jus life may be said to be a worshipper of his duty, his country and so of God himself by his work. In short, real worship of God does not consist in the set forms and formalities of worship. It lies in doing one's own duty with devotion without a selfish motive and doing it for the sake of the nation, the people and the good of humanity.

■　■

43. Nationalization of Industries

Strictly speakeing, this topic belongs to the field of politics and economics but it has aroused nation-wide interest throughout the country as it affects every citizen Nationafeaion is "the process by which organization and industries managed by individuals or Joint-stock companies are t?., .en over by the state. In other words, it means that the state controls and owns the mots prominent of production, industries and business. Such nationalization of industries is an important step towards establishing a socialistic pattern in a country.

But in India, nationalisation of industries is not yet on a complete socialistic pattern. In socialism all means of production are in the hands of the state and no private enterprise is allowed. In India, however, we have a mixed Economy. Certain industries are managed completely by the government (like post, telegraph, etc.). There are some others which were once in the hands of individuals or joint stock companies. They have now been taken over by the state through the process of nationalisation. The railways were once joint stock companies and are now a part of public sector. So are the State Transport and Life Insurance business. However, in certain sector, private industries and public sector industries work *side by side*. The iron and steel industies are an example of such co-existance.

The main argument in favour of nationalisation is the following. In every privately owned industry, the profits go to owner or the shareholders of the joint stock company. Such profits are of no use or service to the common people at all. The owners manage these private industries so as to make the maximum profits out of the business and usually pay little attention to the workers. In a nationalised industry, the profit motive is not very important. It aims at producing the things which the country needs and at giving a square deal to the workers and looking after their needs like housing, medical attention etc. Whatever profits are made are 'ploughed back' or invested in the industry itself to make it more efficient or to expand it so as to give employment to more people. The profits which remain over and above, are used for the good of the common people in the country. Nationalised industries thus have no temptation to resort to unfair means like hoarding, cutting down production, paying low wages etc. in order to increase the profits of the owners. More over, some industries can expand only if they are nationalised because the nation alone can provide the vast capital which such industries may require.

The Air transport is an example of such a necessity No Indian individual owner or even a joint stock company can afford to buy and maintain a fleet of huge Boeing Jet planes which the nationalised Air India international can afford. An argument against nationalisation is that there is' always a loss of efficiency in such industries as neither the managers nor the workers have any personal interest in the business. Secondly, even the customers often do not get the same treatment and attention which they get in a private concern before nationalisation. However, in a country like India, with a policy of socialistic pattern nationalisation, step by step is inevitable.

■   ■

44. Cottage Industries in India

Cottage Industries are industries which are carried out on a small scale by a few workers in their own homes or cottages. In a sense, such cottage industries have been in existence from ancient times throughout the ages. However, coming ofc- the Industrial revolution by the middle of the 18th century divided all industries into two divisions 1) The industries in which there was mass production in big mills and factories using huge and costly machinary. 2) The smaller industries in which the workers used their man-power only and produced a smaller quantity of goods, independantly. For some time, both these kinds of industries ran side by side, and even now there are some that do so. For example a shoemaker or a worker in leather may produce shoes in his cottage working at each pair with his own hands. At the same time, there are big factories producing thousands of pairs of shoes every day.

Thus it is clear that cottage industries cannot compete with the mass-produced goods from factories in quanatity and even in price. Mass production reduces the price level but an independent worker in a cottage will find it uneconomical. So, modern cottage industries are now turning away from the production of goods already being turned out by factories. They are creating an independant market for the special kinds of goods which the factories cannot produce, e.g. the handlooms are used for production of beautiful and artistic woollen and silk shawls, embroidered sarees with gold and silver lace, artistic objects made of sandal wood, ivory, gold, silver, brass and copper.

However, cottage industries should not be considered only from the point of the production of articlels for common use. A more important consideration is the human element. Cottage industries can support the whole family working in the happy surrounding of home life and enjoying the work. This joy in work is impossible if the same worker becomes a labourer in a big factory where he has no personality or individual existence at all. There is little room for special and individual skills in factories where all the products must be uniform. In cottage industries the worker is free to have variety, skill, and excellence to his hearts content.

Even the government has recognised the importance of cottage industries and have given these a place in the community projects and rural uplift schemes. Capital and technical assistance are now provided by the government for cottage industries like hand made paper, bee keeping, metal-ware work, handloom products etc. Some state governments have even reserved certain products for cottage industries only and have forbidden the use of machinary on a factory scale in these. Such industries are the coloured saree industries, the bidi industries, etc. Thus, cottage industries cannot produce goods on a vast scale like the factories, but their products have greater artistic excellence and a human and individual touch not found in mass produced things from factories. What is more important, they provide a welcome source of work and profit to the workers in villages and thus become an important source of social good and social well being.

■　■

45. On Superstitions

Superstitions are descreibed as blind beleif or faith without proof or evidence, this however is a very general description and is equally applicable even to moral and spiritual articles of faith as belief in God, in goodness, mercy, charity, peace etc. Superstitions have a more restricted meaning. They are a special group of beliefs in which the belief is not only without proof but which is purposely maintained in an obstinate manner, secondly, unlike the beleifs in moral and spiritual principles, such superstitions can lead to a lot of evil and harm. That is why all religious and moral teachers have earnestly advocated that people should give up superstitions.

Thus superstitions can be roughly divided into two groups. The first one is that of the superstitions which may appear to be silly, unreasonable but which do not do much harm. So, these can be taken lightly. They can be gradually removed by gentle satire, mockery, and ridicule and do not require any stronger measures. Examples of such superstitions can be found in plenty not only in India but even in the western nations in spite of their scientific out-look. A cat crossing the path, an owl sitting on one's house are supposed to bring ill luck. Flickering of the left eyelid, fall of a lizard on the body etc. are also believed to be signs of some unfavourable event in the future. In western countries also, the figure 13 and Friday are supposed to be unlucky. Lighting three cigarattes from one match, breaking of a mirror, walking under a ladder are also supposed to bring bad luck. All these can be called superstitions because bey have abosolutely no foundation of logical or scientific reason behind them. Yet, these superstitions _are harmless and can be looked upon with mild amusement and not with strong disapproval.

But this is not the case with superstitions of the second group which are far more serious and even dangerous for society. Past History of the west and the east are full of horrible stories of persecution of persons who were supposed to be witches or persons in league with the Devil. Superstitious people believed that such persons could bring about diseases and even death for the persons whom they hated. So, when a child or a grown person fell ill suddenly, some old woman was supposed to have cast an evil spell on him. She was dragged out and persecuted and sometimes even^burnt alive. Mad persons were supposed to be possessed by the'Devil and were whipped and branded with hot irons so as to drive the Devil away. Little children were buried alive under the foundations and bridges to make these firm. Hundreds of goats, cocks were sacrificed when some disease like the small-pox invaded a village. Even human sacrifice before Gods was not unknown under the false idea that it would please the God and bring wealth and prosperity to the person making the sacrifice.

Needless to say, all these beliefs had no truth in them at all. They were superstitions, but they continued for centuries and did untold harm, So, it is best to think clearly before accepting any such belief that may bring some harm to some one must be absolutely set aside, however popular it might be.

■ ■

46. Atomic Energy a blessing or a curse

19th century was the age of steam. Early part of the 20th century was the age of Electricity; but the later part of this century is the age of Atomic energy. To-day, Atomic energy is far more powerful source than steam, electricity or any other source of energy known to man.

For ages an Atom was supposed to be the smallest unit of matter. Then at the end of the 19th century, Thompsom, later Lord Rutherford, showed that the Atom itself was made up of smaller units called the Protons Electrons and Neotrons. These are particles of positive, negative and no charge, revolving round a solid core (called a Nucleus) Every substance has its own Atomic structure. By knocking some atoms we can change one substance into another. Thus, Atoms of Radium constantly passing off turn the substance into lead.

The next important discovery was that it was possible to break up the solid Nucleus of .a substance by bombarding it with a stream of neutrons. The energy locked up in the atom can thus be realised when the atom is disintegrated or broken up. Physics states that nothing is ever destroyed; it only changes from one form to another. Einstein proved mathematically by his formula that if one atom is completely destroyed it will produce tremendous energy (The square of Mass X the velocity of light) This theory was to be proved by actual experiment. The German, English and American scientists were all trying to make use of it to produce the Atom Bomb. Hitler was constantly talking of his "Secret weapon" which would change defeat into victory once Germany could have it. But Hitler's persecutions drove away the Jewish scientists into America, and Germany could not make the Atom Bomb and had to surrender.

By 1944 Einstein, Oppenheimer, Fermi and other scientists wrote a letter to President Roosevelt saying that they were now ready to create a tremendously effective Atom Bomb if it was necessary for the defence of Democracy. At that time war with Japan was costing thousands of lives, and would continue to do so if the war continued. The only remedy was to bring it to sudden end by making Japan surrender.

The first Atom Bomb was tested on the pacific island of Bikini, and the second in the desert of Mexico. Both showed the terrible power of destruction. So on 8th August 1945 the First Atom Bomb was dropped on the Japanese city of Hiroshima and then the second on the city of Nagasaki. Each bomb killed about 80,000 people at once and thousands later by a slow and painful process of disintegration of tissues.

The two bombs brought about the surrender of Japan but created a terrible problem for the whole mankind. Later research developed even more terrible types of Hydrogen and Cobalt bombs, far more powerful than the first Atom Bombs. A few such bombs can destroy a whole population of a country, soldiers, civilians, animals and birds. Men like Bretrand Russell warned humanity that it was likely that the whole of humanity might be wiped out from the surface of the earth if many Atom Bombs were dropped at the same time, thus producing a continuous chain-reaction of disintegration and destruction. So, efforts are no^ being made to make treaties banning atomic weapons and promising not to use them. It is however doubtful how far these will be honoured in the case of the Third world war.

All this may make most people think that Atomic energy is a curse and should be banned once and for all. But this is not so. Atomic Fission (breaking up) has placed a very powerful energy in the hands of man. It is for him to make a good or bad use of it. This energy will provide power to man kind in future when the stocks of Coal, Oil, wood will be exhausted. Atomic energy has been successfully used to drive engines and to produce Electricity. The submarine *Nautilus* has circled the whole world only on one pound of Uranium as a fuel through the Atomic energy provided by it. The Atomic reactor called Apsara at Tarapore in India is already producing thousands of megawatts of electric energy. The spaceships using Atomic energy can go out to reach distant planets like Mars and Venus.

Even in the field of Medicine and Agriculture, Atomic energy is now being used for constructive purposes.- In future, Trains, ships submarines etc. will be powered by Atomic energy. Radio-active substances like Radium are being used to burn out the tissues of Cancer. The Atomic clock is supposed to be the most accurate and the Geiger counter can count the age of any substance, however old, by measuring radio-activity. Unlike other fuels like coal, oil, petrol electricity, Atomic energy does not require big masses of raw materials to produce it. A few pounds of a natural substance like Uranium or Plutonium can produce tremendous energy without harmful by products like smoke, harmful chemicals etc.

Thus, Atomic energy is a great gift given to man. It has given him almost God-like power. However, it is left to his wisdom whether to use it like a god for the good of humanity or like a Devil for destruction. It can be a blessing or a curse according to the purpose for which it is used.

■　■

47. Students and social service

It is sometime said that modern students have no sense of social responsibility. It may be true in the case of some students who care only for amusement and the pleasures of their youth, but by and large, and majority are willing to do something for society. The trouble is that they do not find good leadership among themselves or their teachers who would use their enthusiasm in the right direction. When such leadership is there, students have always shown that they have played their part with distinction.

To go back to the recent past, the part played by students in the freedom movement has been written in letters of gold in the struggle of independence. Even young boys of 14 and 15 held on to the national flag in spite of lathi charge and even died in firing. Students in Sindh, Gujrat, U. P. and Bengal suffered wounds and even death while trying to persuade the fighters during communal riots. In the post-partition riots, there were hundreds and thousands of young men and even boys from voluntery organizations (mostly college students) who helped to organize the refugee camps, to protect them and to provide for their needs.

Even in the recent past, during natural calamities like the flood of Panshet, the earthquake of Koyana, the festivals like that of Ganapati, the annual fairs and processions etc, batches of students worked day and night to help the authorities. They collect money, clothes, food etc. for distribution among the victims of flood and eqrthquake.

However, such services for social good must be properly organised. The students must receive intensive training in order to perform social service in an effective manner. If this is not done, they usually lose the freshness and enthusiasm within a short time and very little remains to be shown as a permanent record of their service.

Some efforts in this direction are being made, however they are not yet enough. The gpvernment has made it compulsory for fresh medical graduates to spend one year in the villages before they can claim the right to practice in the cities. It will probably be made compulsory for some other branches also to be of service to the society, especially in the villages before they will be allowed to work for themselves.

Social services today are rapidly becoming a kind of specialised branch of knowledge like medicine. Though there is room in it for volentery, part-time and occasional work by students, serious work in this direction will have to be done by persons specially trained for this purpose. We would like to draw the attention of the students who have a liking for social service to undergo regular training in institutes like the Tata school of .Social service in Bombay or the Karve Institute if Social' service in Poona. In addition to this training, youth and service camps are held every year all over India where young men and women are invited to serve the villagers and the poor farmers. Service of humanity is a service of God and students must take up their share in this great and necessary work.

■ ■

48. 'Power corrupts and absolute power corrupts absolutely.'

This remark was made by a great English politician named Lord Bryce. It contains an important truth though it does contain some controversial element in it also. What Lord Bryce wanted to say was that any kind of power without proper check or control has a tendency of corrupting- or spoiling the standard of purity of person. One or two examples will make this point quite clear.

In the matters of finance and commerce, men have to deal with very large sums of money. These transactions are recorded by the man who keeps the accounts. Yet the matters are not left entirely under the control of the accountant. Another officer called the Auditor is appointed to examine these records and check them periodicaly. He has to see that the power given to the accountant is not abused and used for corruption. It is easy to see that if such a control is not exercised, unchecked power may easily lead to corruption and misappropriation of money. Over and above the Internal auditor there is the government auditor or a similar authority to see that the auditor and the accountant do not make a common cause and abuse their power.

In the field of law also, no absolute power is given to the officers of law. A man who suspects a miscarriage of justice, can go from an ordinary court to the High Court and as a last resort may even appeal to the President of India to intervene. This control keeps the machinary of the law and finance under proper conditions.

However, the statement made by Lord Bryce has a special

application in the field of politics. History is full of examples that go to show that dictators and kings who had absolute power, without any control by the people have played havoc. There have been terrible monsters of violence like Changiz Khan, Nadir Shah, who slaughtered thousands mercilessly because they had abosolute power in their hands. Napoleon, Hitler, Mussolini, Stalin were all dictators to whom power was handed over by the people, trustfully. All these dictators first began with the very good intention of making their people and their country rich, happy and strong. However, as time went on their original intention began to be corrupted. They first crushed all those who whould have exercised somecontrol or opposition to them. When all fear of such opposition was gone, they simply ran wild, became mad for power and pleasure and finally brought ruin both on themselves and innocent people who had given the power so trustfully in their hands.

As we said above, there might be exceptions here and there to this rule. In ancient bistory, we find that the kings in those times had absolute power in their hands and yet many of them were really great and good. Kings like Rama, Ashoka, Vikramaditya, Shivaji in the east and Charlmegne, Alfred, Richard I, Queen Elizabeth I In the west are examples how even absolute power could be used for the good of the people. However, It is true that absolute power can tempt even a good man to misuse his position. That is why in modern democracy, a strong opposition is always kept intact to exercise such control over the ruling party. Newspapers also provide a check over the public activities of officers and leaders who have considerable power in their hands. They have thus to be careful in their conduct to escape being exposed and dismissed from power.

49. The role of Science in modern world

This topic is so wide and varied that it will require a volume rather than an essay to exhaust it. However, a few facts of the ways in which science now affects the different forms of human life and society will be enough for our purpose.

At the outset, we must understand that the implications of science in modern times are much wider than those in the past, In the past, science was supposed to be confined to the laboratories and to deal with things like physics and chemistry and biology etc. Its effects were confined to these sciences and to the scientists working in those fields. Now, all that is completely changed. Every activity of human life, in every corner of the earth is affected by the work of science and the scientists. Transport, lightening, Public health, communications, amusements, the cloths we wear, the food we eat, the vessels that we use, the buildings we live inrthese and many other activities are profoundly affected by science. In fact, the very existence of the modern conditions in the department of life refferred to above can be said to exist due to the work of science and the scientists. If the scientists had not made the discovries, these ways of life today could never have come into existance e. g. the single discovery of a spinning and weaving machine suddenly changed the age-long ways of cloth industry from a handicraft to the mass-production of cloth in mills.

Science has not affected only the physical activities and ways of human life. It has influenced even the minds and thoughts of humanity. The discoveries of Galileo, and Copernicus, later on those of James Jeans, Eddington, Einstein, Hoyle etc. have changed and very conception of the univers and the laws which govern it. The reasearches of Darwin, Lyall, Huxley, Mendel and other Biologists have actually changed our old ideas about the creation of man and other animals and the ways of human body and the mind.

In this way, science in the past has almost reshaped and reorganised human life and human activities Within a short period of about hundred and fifteen years, enough work was done by science to changed the ways of humanlife which had existed for thousands and thousands of years in the past.

Much of this work is good no doubt. But lately some discoveries of science have been so disturbing that even great thinkers have begun to doubt whether the role of science has been really so beneficial for man. The invention of the Atom and Hydrogen bombs, nerve gas, germ warfare, Psychological war, brain washing, experiments for producing life artificially have very dangerous implications for the whole of humanity. Some thinkers even see the possibility of the complete destruction of all human and animal life on the earth or the enslavement of all human beings by a few scientist-dictators in distant future. So they cry a halt to the further encroachments of science in the field of human life. This is however a counsel of despair. Under proper guidance and direction towards human happiness and freedom, science can play a very important part in turning this earth into another heaven.

50. The problem of umemployment

The problem of unemployment is one of the burning topics of today. Much of the dissatisfaction and discontent among the people, especially the educated young people is due to unemployment. Though some steps to relieve this state are being taken, they are not enough to solve it completely. Patch work and hap-hazard measures will never solve the problem unless the very fundamental conditions are changed. So, it is necessary first to consider the problem and its extent, systematically.

The turn unemployment does not merely mean not being able to get a job. It means that the state in which a person who is willing and capable of doing the proper kind of job, is not able to get one in spite of his efforts and qualifications. The fitness of the man may be physical or intellectual. We do not call a lame or a blind man or a professional begger unemployed simply because he does not do any work.

The simplest economic reason for umemployment for workers in any field of work is that the supply is more than the demand. It is easy to see how this has happened even in specialized and technical fields like that of engineers. Just a few years back, makers of the five years plan had declared that thousands and thousands of engineers would be required to manage the various development schemes of the country. New colleges and institutes of engineering were opened and thousands of engineering graduates and diploma holders were turned out. Suddenly it was discovered that there was some mistake in the calculation and not all these people would be required for the jobs in hand. So, we have seen the strange sight of even diploma holders and graduates in engineering, going about umemployed and asking for jobs even of clerks! This is even more so for arts and science graduates. Some of these have been glad enough to work as primary teachers where S.S.C. and even lower qualifications are needed. Some times back there was a sight even of graduates polishing shoes in streets in some cities. The government cannot be expected to find a job for every student that comes out of the college. It is no use trying to tear up or burn the degree because it cannot provide a job.

It has been said that an umemployed man is an unemployable man. This mejins that one who' remains umemployed must be a man who .cannot or will not do some kind of work which he can get. Most people want 'White collar' jobs where they can work at a table at ease. Strangely enough. While the number of the unemployed graduates is rising, there is an acute shortage of qualified and hard working artisans like turners, fitters, plumbers, carpenters, masons, electricians, welders, nurses, doctors, motor mechanics, industrial-chemists, etc. Several of these jobs pay much more than the jobs of clerks or junior officers and yet they are not popular because they require hard physical labour. It is necessary therefore that our students should change their attitude towards work and their careers if they want to save themselves from umemployment. Similarly, it requires a change in the social and family attitude towards job. Our young men must now change their home-keeping habits and must be ready to go to any corner of our country and even to places beyond the seas for their career. There is much demand for really qualified teachers, right from the primary to the college level in Asian and African countries like Egypt, Etheopia, Kuwait, Malaya, etc. But not many of our young men (at least from Maharashtra) are interested in these jobs. Same is the case with professions like nursing, in case of young ladies from this part of the country.

Remedies for umemployment on a public scale have been already proposed. Growth of industrilization will provide thousands with employment provided they are willing to do any work which falls to their hands. New government projects in next five years plan will 'be able to absorb more and more technically trained persons. Opening of new schools, in villages and towns, new centres for social welfare and community projects will give employment to thousands who are prepared to go and live in the villages, The governments are actually intersted in helping the educated people who are willing to start independent industries, business, small scale cottage industries. Nationalised banks are coming forward to give them loans on favourable terms, to meet their requirements. It is however necessary that the pefople should change their ways of thinking and be prepared to take initative in business, industries, agriculture or any new scheme instead of merely running after safe jobs.

Thus, we see that the problem of umemployment is a very complex one and is a result of social, economic, political and human factors. It has been there in our country since the times of the British and will not be quickly solved even after independence. It must be boldly faced by our young men as a challenge. They must work together with the forces of the government, industries and even of international bodies whole heartedly to wipe out this situation. Then the problem will be solved as it is now solved by countries like West-Germany, England and Japan.

POINTS FOR ESSAY-WRITING

(It is rightly said that Essay-writing cannot be taught; it has to be *learnt.* This means that one cannot learn the Art of Essay-writing merely by reading essay written by others. He must practise writing essays. One cannot learn to swim merely by reading how to swim, one has to jump into water and practise swimming. Students have already read some specimens of various kinds of Essays in the previous pages. Let them now turn to writing their own essays. To help them in doing so, we given them a few points or hints which will give them enough material for writing these essays.)

1. Descriptive and Narrative Essays

1. *Diwali or the Festival of Lights*

Points- When does the Diwali come? — The scene of the season-reasons for rejoicing — the mythological stories about the festival — the first day — Dhan trayodashi — the second day — the early baths — crackers — sweets — the third day, the main day — worship of the Goddess of wealth — The Bhaubeej or the Brother's day — its importance to family life — Conclusion — importance of such festivals.

2. Rubber and its uses

It is a Juice of trees in Congo and Amazon basin — how was it discovered — the early uses of rubber — Raw rubber or Latex — cured rubber — Used for sports — balls, balloons, toys — chief uses — rubber wheels and tubes for vehicles — gloves and tubes used in surgery — Synthetic or artificial rubber — Rubber industry in India — bags, shoes, foam mattresses and pillows. One of the most useful and comforting articles used in modern civilesed life.

3. The Autobiography of a school blackboard

How the writer came to learn the account — The origin in the form of a tree in the forest — it is cut down — made into planks — taken to a city — stocked in a timber yard — What happened to others — this board taken to a school — - the carpenter makes a blackboard — a black coating applied to the surface — The first day in the class — how boys made use of it for mischief — used for notices
— sums in mathematics — rubbed clean at the end of the day — teaches but learns nothing itself — blank for ever.

4. A visit to a Zoo

Zoo a short form of Zoological garden — wild animals kept in cages and in the open — Occasion for the visit — persons in the party — Lions — tigers — wolves — crocodiles — monkeys — fun at the cages — giraffes and elephants — kangaroos — birds of various kinds — an enjoyable and instructive expience.

5. An Indian Village

Where the village is situated — the surroundings — the entrance — the small market place — the temples — the village tank or well — the houses of the farmers — the house of the very poor — the village school — the village Panchayat

— house — the village Patel •— The schoolmaster speeks — The entertainments in the village — festivals -* difficulties of the future of the villge.

6. Visit to a fair

Occasion of the fair — the places — the shops — the places of amusement the roundabouts — the giantwheel — the daring motorcyclists in a well — the photographers — the toysellers — the hawkers of sweets, the temple — the singers and devotees — the pickpockets and vagabonds — Villagers from far and wide — the uses of such fairs — Cattle fairs — government stalls — useful and instructive. A social institution from ancient days — it should continuine a new form.

7. A cricket match

The occasion — the two teams — some prominent players, the preparation for the match — the toss — the first batsmen — their dismissal, some interesting incidents — the total — the opposite team starts batting — an early fall of wickets — how it was stopped — a fine hitter — the total second innings of both sides — the exciting finish — a win for your team — the prize distribution — a procession of the victorious team.

8. Your favourite book

Name of the author, when was it published — what is the subjuctmatter of that book — the description of the contents if a novel, give the story in short — the leading characters humour. Pathos etc. if a book with some problem or description state the leading ideas and stress their importance
— conclude by recommending others to read the book for pleasure and profit.

9. The market place in a city

The attractive appearance of the shops — the various types of shops — different kinds of goods in the shopwindows — the crowds of men and women looking at the goods and entering the shops — modern art of window — dressing and salesmanship — the appearance of a typical shopkeeper — his manner of receiving a customer — bargaining, persuading the customer to buy — A Departmental Store — smaller shops at the back — their purpose and usefulness — the shops reflect the prosperity or otherwise of a country.

10. My school or My College

Name *of* the institution — why the name stands for — The Organization which runs the school or the College — how old — description of the building — the class rooms — the library — the teachers, room — the Gymktfana and the playing fields — some remarks about the Headmaster or the Principal — some notable teachers or professors who have interested you — Your own experiences in the institution — the final impression you will carry in life.

11. Your favourite hobby

What is a hobby? advantages of having a hobby — entertainment as well as knowledge or exercise — Social interest or contacts some kinds of hobbies — stamp collecting, music, playing games, card playing, reading, going for on trips, photography, learning new languages, writing stories, sketches etc.— (give details) The joy of new ideas and experiences — making new acquaintances — The need to keep hobby from being too serious — it must not interfere with the serious work in life.

12. The seasons in India

Seasons which are the chief ones — Summer, the Rainy season and the Winter. — A brief description of each of them

— sub-divisions — the spring season — the Autumn— the October heat. The six seasons according to old Indian calendar — The Four seasons in the western countries — the spring — the summer the autumn and the winter. References to the seasons in poetry or prose you have read — describe one natural scene changing *its* appearance through these seasons.

13. *A famous building you have seen*
Name of the building — who built it? when? where is it situated the places round about it — Your journey to it — the first impression — the detailed description of the building — the' scene which can be seen from it — the use to which it was put in the past — the use now, if any — your thoughts on seeing the building — the need of preserving such old and famous building they are-a part of the cultural heritage of a nation.

14. *A Printing Press*
The occasion of your visit — the reception room — the typecomposing hall — the method of setting types — the typecasting room — the hand press — proof correcting— the printing machine — Treydle, Cylinder or Rotory — The block making section the binding section — the showroom— the sales department — importance of such printing presses in modern age. Your thoughts and impressions.

15. *A riot*
The occasion of the riot — The rumours and the faint hints the preparations of both the parties in secret — the crowds in the streets — the police precautions — The incident that sat off the spark of the riot — where the riot first began — the progress, attacks in the lanes — on the high road — appearance of the police — the lathi charge — Tear gas — firing —the wounded taken to the Hospital — declaration of section 144. the streets deserted — the loss of

life and property — need to avoid riots.

16. Exhibition

1. What are exhibitions - their value as entertainment, educational commercial, social, political cultural etc.

2. Difference between a fair and an exhibition. No religious signiture.

3. Types of exhibitions — industrial, commercial, agricultural, Photographical, Arts and crafts, dramatic, cinematographic etc.

4. Some great International exhibition — Wembly, Tokyo, Munich, Delhi etc.

5. Conclusion — the usefulness of exhibitions — international and cultural relationships.

17. Writting instruments old and new

1. Oldest writing instruments — read pens, goose feather pens, coal sticks, thick needles to carve tha plam leaves etc.

2. The steel pens with a split nib — Removable nibs for writing on paper, vellum, brushes for painting letters as in china.

3. Discovery of the fountain pens in 19th century.

4. Various methods of filling in ink. 4

5. The stylo pen with a a needle point in the place of a nib.

6. The ball — point pen with thick ink discovered in the second world war — its advantages — its disadvantages-

7. Why ball point pens are not allowed for cheques and signatures by the post and Government.

18. Autobiography of a pet dog

The early days of the dog — its difficulties and danger in life — its escapes — its first master, a boy — the life in a poor house — it is driven away by the mother of the boy as it requires much- food — it is on the point of starvation — the present owner takes pity on it and brings it home — It keeps cldse to the owner and saves it from danger — now lying at the foot of the bed — the owner and saves it from danger — now lying at the foot of the bed — the owner sees it in his dream and learns these facts from him.

19. A Weekly bazzar in a small torni

Your visit to a small town in the vacation — You are roused by sudden noises one early morning on sunday — The scene from your window — Big/icrowds are gathering — various stalls on the footpaths —.You go out with your local friends — various lanes with different types of goods — vegetable — cloth — sweets — bangles and trinkets — toys — foodgrains — milk butter and ghee — fruits, stalls for refreshments etc. — The people who visit these bazzars — the usefulness of these for villagers living far away from the town markets.

20. A Sudden flood

The memory of the Panshet Flood — Constant rains for some days — rising of water level — still the people did not care much — the water reaches the first streets — men and boys move about as if it is fun — the police give the first warning of the bursting of the dam — schools are let off — people in low lying are advised to leave — the flood water reaches the houses and rises rapidly — The Khadakwasala dam bursts — sudden further rise of water — many houses collapse — man and animals carried away water enters the second stories of houses — great alarm in the city — water, electricity cut off — a dark and terrible night — the water recedes — the pitiful sights in the streets — homeless people housed in schools and colleges — food and clothes distributed — problem of finding accomodation for these new colonies being formed a memory never to be forgotten.

■ ■

Stage II
Intermediate — Reflective essays

21.Reading of novels

How and why novels are so popular ?— your personal experience — arguments against reading novels — waste of time, showing a false world, false values of life, types of novels — romantic, realistic, adventure — novels etc. Advantaages of reading novels — amusement, getting experience of life at second hand. — conclusion — a proper choice of novels must be made — such reading should be in moderation.

22.The Radio — *its use and abuse*

Radio first called wireless telegraphy invented by the Italian scientist Marconi — Fleming invents the value giving human voice and sounds to the wireless signals — cheap radio transistor radio — its appeal to the listeners — brings great singers and artists to our room — a nuisance when it is turned on too loudly — variety of programmes — Music, Gramo-phone records — Radio Ceylon, Vividh-Bharati — nuisance of — advertisements — sports commentaries — interviews, complaints — suggestions for improvement.

23. *Students and social service*

A common misconception that such service is not for students — but they can do much good — their energy must be rightly directed — Best time for such service, the vacations — socil service camps to be held — kinds of service, — cleaning the village, teaching, medical attendance, eye and teeth camps managed by students, entertainments, travelling cinemas with lecturers on useful subjects. Such service will remove the wrong image of students now in public mind.

24. *Value of Hope in life*

Modern tendency of disillusionment and frustration — many young men feel life to be hopeless — difference between hope and ambition — why hopes are disappointed — need so keep with in th£ limits of attainment — Examples of men who succeeded because they never lost hope in difficulties — king Bruce of Scotland, Rana pratap, Shivaji, Gandhiji Columbus, Edison etc. warning against hoping for too much and losing hope quickly at the first touch of bad luck. While there is life, there should be hope.

25. *The use of Libraries*

Libraries in the past, Handwritten books stored princes and scholars, world famous libraries, the Badlein at Oxford. The paris national library; the Library of the congress in America. National library in Calcutta. Different kind of libraries, books, manuscripts, films, records, pictures, documents Travelling libraries, School and College libraries.

Proper use to be made of libraries — Bad habit of some readers— tearing out pages, pictures etc-loss of valuable books, bad impression in foreign countries if done by Indian students— Proper knowledge of classification of books and their arrangement-knowing what to read for each subject. Building a small private library possible for each one if properly provided for.

26. Qualities of a good citizen

Science of citizenship now called Civics — Its importance— Rights of citizen — Housing, water, light, sanitation, use of parts hospitals, streets, street lighting-Public conveniences like urinals, swimming pools, dispensaries etc— In return, some duties necessary — paying taxes — keeping the city clean — obeying the laws, Actions against good citizenship to be avoided e.g. making too much noise, throwing dirt in the streets, smoke and other pollution to be avoided.

27. Dangers of smoking

Smoking uses tobaco in various forms — Bidis. cigarettes cigars, hoka, pipe, chewing tobacco, taking snuff etc — reasons of its popularity — effect of tobacco on nerves — nicotine a mild soother of nerves. The advantage set off by many disadvantages-irritates the throat, spoils the taste, damages the lungs. Graetest danger — too much smoking makes cancer of the lung possible. Chewing tobacco and keeping a lump of tobacco in the mouth inclines to encourage the cancer of the mouth and tongue. Smoking best avoided for reasons of health — it should not be taken up for fashion.

28. On Temperance (Dangers of drinking alchohol)

Meaning of the word temperance — Restraint in drinking liquor, food, behaviour* etc. Particularly used now for keeping away from liquior — Drinking condemened by several religions also by medical science — Alchohol a drug for stimulation and warmth — to be used for medical purposes only — evils results wine misused — loss of control over speech and behaviour — followed by severe headache — leads to diseases of the liver — becomes a fixed habit — has destroyed the happiness of hundreds of families — So, it is best to keep away from it — Policy of prohibition however not very successful. Persuasion and pointing out the evils the best way.

29. On Courage

What is courage — Two of courages — physical and moral — give example of each — which is the greater of the two? the moral — say why — why courage is rare? fear mostly due to imagination — Proper knowledge will lead to courage in facing it. Proper training can be given from school days- Hunting, shooting — lathi play, self-defence will give one courage — courage should not lead to rashness and inviting danger purposely — example. Conclusion — courage necessary for successful life.

30. Use and abuse of the cinema

Cinema a recent invention — Lumiere in France — Edison in America, White in England developed it. Phalke in India produced the first film — The silent films — the Talkies— the 3 D. Films — Cinemascope. Main purpose — entertainment — can also be used for intstrucfion, information, permanent record of memorable events — Abuse-crime pictures— false glamour imitating Cinema stars romantic craze for love craze for the cinema makes young people disinclined to do hard work and live a contented life. Conclusion — Seeing good pictures in moderation one of the blessings of modern civilised life.

31. On Duty

What is duty — difference between duty and compulsion of task — types of duty — family, society, Nation and humanity — all duties rising one over the other besides personal interest — give examples of each type — returns for duty done — office, business, army, nevy etc. — Standards higher than such paid duty — ideal of Geeta — doing duty without expecting return — difficult — ideal but the highest — Great men like Vivekanand, Gandhi, Christ, Buddha all famous for doing their duty for the good of all humanity. Conclusion — Each one shuld do his duty to the best of his ability — Satisfaction after this is the best reward.

32. We live in deeds and not in years

Meaning of this proverb — Not to be taken literally — Mere long life not worth — but merit, good deeds, happiness, service etc. worth more than mere long life — examples of long but unhappy life through paralysis, asthama, madness etc. not worth while examples of great men who lived a short but useful life — Christ Byron, Keats, Shelley, Rupert Brook great poets who died young. This does not mean that long life is not worth having — the real significance of the saying.

33. The pen is mightier tuaa the sword

The meaning and significance of the proverb — not always true, literally — Pen standing for writing in various forms, mainly literature, laws, religion etc — Sword standing for military might, physical strength etc. Intellectual power superior to mere brute strength — examples in wrestling games, battles, social life etc. Sword destroys but the pen or literature creates new way of life — However, the two are not mutually exclusive — in modern National life. Both are necessary.

34. Community projects

Meaning of the phrase — village uplift and the betterment of the communities which are backward — Lead given by Gandhiji in his village reconstruction policy — charkha, hand-loom weaving, poultry keeping, bee keeping etc. Bhoodan movements of Vinoba — Gramsevaks — Village Panchayats — soil testing advice to the farmers about agriculture — village co-operative stores for seeds, fertilisers wells, co-operative housing — sanitation water supply — tube wells bunding of fields. Education, transport. The final aim to bring the advantages of town life to the villages.

■　■

110

State III

Reflective, Expository and Argumentative
essays

35.*Old order changes yielding place to new*

A line from Tennyson — the meaning to of the line — a law of life — Everything is in a constant state of change — give examples — the body, the mind, water, light, health, our activities fashions, manners, To stay unchanged like stagnant water is too hot — Even good things like music, literature have to change slightly and to get better or undergo some variation — examples desire for a holiday, a journey, games, change of furniture in the house, change of food — Conclusion one must not be in a fixed routine of life and action.

36.*The child is father of the man*

A line from Wordsworth's poem 'My heart leaps up' At first sight this seems to be a strange statement — Real meaning — the child shows what the grown up man is likely to be — ' Childhood shows the man as morning shows the day' (Milton) Examples of the early signs of greatness —

The childhood of Shivaji, Nelson, Lokamanya Tilak etc. —
However the proverb is not always true — Some men develop
late — childhood quite common — place examples —
Gandhiji, Nehru, Churchill etc. Impressions of childhood
very strong and easily made they continue through the life
— Conclusion — duty of parents tb give proper training to
children, physical and mental and moral for future success.

37.Necessity is the mother of invention

A great truth in simple words — Invention or new ways
of action seldom come those who do not feel the need of
these. One tries various, ways and succeeds when it becomes
absolutely necessary —(Robinson Crusoe learns to build a
hut, stitch clothes, plant crops, bake bread, make pots and
furniture without any training. Human civilization a record
of inventions when they were necessary — agriculture,
architecture writing, music etc. — Some inventions lay
unused when there was no necessity for them — designs of
aeroplanes by Leonardo da Vinci, submarine, tanks etc.
necessity for rapid transport — made Railways possible.
Second world war German bombing brought the invention
of Radar, Atom Bomb to win the war etc.

38.Broadcasting

A short sketch of the origin — Hertzian waves —
Marconi's success in transmitting telegraphic messages
without wires — Fleming's discovery of the valve — Modern
all wave radio — Talk and music from all parts of the world
— discovery of the transistor made radios very cheap — the
educational value of the radio — entertainment — music,
plays, sketches, warning in times of danger. Some
disadvantages — constant noise — advertisements as on
'Radio ceylon' and ' Vividh Bharati,' However, the blessing
for outweight the few disadvantages.

39. On Famines

Causes of famines - failure of rains, too much of rains, Locusts, Prevention almost impossible — measures like artificial rain still in experimental stage. Measures to help the people are possible — providing tube wells — water in tankers — famine relief works for the farmers — distribution of food grains — fodder for the animals, digging tanks, making roads etc to give employment to the villagers importing grains milk powder for children, danger of epidemics bring famine — measures to meet this threat, conclusion — adequate stocks of grain and fodder should be kept and moved on to famine — struck places, Bunding of lands growing trees for encouraging rain storing of water in tanker.

40. Sufferings of the Harijaas

Harijans formerly called the Uutouchables — the reason — the old social order based on four castes — those outside these were the untouchables — doing dirty but necessary work for the good of the society — Neglected group of society — saints in India tried to make the people consious of the unjust treatment of Harijans — attempts at justice — not much success — Mahatma Fule, Ambedkar, Greatest name — that of Gandhiji — his teachings largely effective. Untouchability now a crime — yet in villages still some prejudice against Harijans exists — equality in services — hotels and restaurants, now by law. Spread of education, habits of cleanliness, necessary for a fair deal to the Harijans. Bitterness and anger of little use. Duty of the public to the Harijans never t6 be forgotten.

41.Should Prohibition be enforced by law all over India?

What does the word prohibition stand for — Prohibiting wines — religious rules in Hindu and Mohomedan religions Excess of liqueur similarly condemned by all moral and religious rules — Laws against drunkenness present in all countries — Then why prohibition ? — moderate drinking gradually leads to excess. So, even moderate drinking must be stopped — This is the view of prohibition — Good result if prohibition is seriously observed and enforced. Not there are many loopholes in law and the observation of laws, smuggling of liquor — illegal preparation of liquor in huts — bribery of policemen and officers — So, some states have now modified prohibition — Prohibition can be best enforced by educating people about the evils of drink and not by mere legal rules.

42.Plain living and high thinking

Explain both terms, plain living and high thinking — Plain living does not mean living like a beggar, but without undue luxuries or vices. High thinking means rising above the selfish and material values of life. It is the ideal of service and sacrifice — Give on example of a selfish and pleasure loving man and one of a man of high thinking Gandhiji, Vivekananda and best examples of the latter — What compensation does a plain living give? What are the punishments and disappointments of a life of mere luxury? Conclusion — Final judgements of man based on what he lives for, and how he lives;for others.

43.What is preferable ? health or wealth ?

A question difficult to answer — Usual answer — health. Wealth can provide medicines and hospital care but hot real health. But wealth is also not to be carelessly dismissed — Thousands of healthy men live in unhappiness throughout life — Wealth can be inherited but also won by health, knowledge and hard work, such wealth is worth baving — Other side — only wisdom, health or scholarship without any wealth is often disregarded. Conclusion — Best to aim at both. But if only one is possible, one should choose health and then use it to get wealth.

44.Hero and hero worship

Who is a hero? — old idea of an hero a great religious leader, a conqueror very brave man. Susch men almost worshipped praised and imitated — modern idea of a hero— a national leader a benefactor of humanity, a great sportsman an actor (Stage or Film) or a great singer. — Such praise or worship — common in the past and the present — Dangers of such worship — blind following as of Hitler. Mussolini led to Fascist rule arid great war and destruction in the second world war. It prevents of people from thinking for themselves or to oppose anything proposed by such heroes. Respect, appreciation Yes; but worship; No.

45.Should there be compulsory military training in India ?

Such training present in America, France etc — Advantages of such training — better discipline — better readiness and fitness for the protection of the country in times of danger

— better effeciency useful iri any profession in life after such training — Other side of the question — compulsion produces dislike and hate-those not fit for training waste money, resources and time of the army — They will never make good or capable soldiers — They will try to escape training by various tricks and excuses — give examples from N.C.C. when it was compulsory — so now it is, made coluntary — conclusion compulsion only in times of emergency-persuasion of the fit and willing the best way.

46.Popular superstitions

Difference between a superstition and true belief — a fact. Give examples of superstitions of the past-witches, possession by the Devil, the number 13 as unlucky, Friday as unlucky, an owl on the house or a cat crossing the path unlucky. Walking under a ladder, breaking of a mirror,

trembling of an eyelid fall of a lizard on the body, a bad
dream, Saturday a bad day for beginning a new work-lighting
three cigarettes from one match etc. — Such beliefs have no
proof — they may result in great harm — burning of witches
in the middle ages ill treatment of the madmen in the past
— Some superstitions harmless e. g. no. 13, Friday or
Saturdays avoided etc. As science advanced, superstitions
will decline.

47. Do we have too many holidays ?

Holidays in the past very few- Sunday in the West a part
of Christian religion the day of rest- Not so in the east in the
past — Our holidays those of religious festivals and visits
of the great Holiday, really holiday — later on the word-
came to mean doing nothing. In India, the number too big
— we combine the western and the eastern both, and waste
our working days — deaths of the great an excuse for a
holiday — not so in the west — hartals — cricket maches
— joy at some success, a day after some celebration, all an
excuse for a holiday — These must be cut down — proper
number of holidays however necessary for health and
efficiency. Cutting short school and College long vacations,
Christmas and Diwali holidays necessary for better and more
work.

48. Wonders of modern science

DivitTe/the essay in wonders of Physics, Chemistry,
Biology transports, atomic science — Physics — worders
of electricity — Telegram, Telephone electric lamps the
cinema, radio, television, Rockets to the moon and Mars
intercontinental missilesupersonic jet planes, submarines etc.
Chemistry — Antibiotics — chemical drugs, plastics,
Synthetic fabrics like Terylene, Nilons Dacron, new metals
like Titanium, Stainless steel etc, synthetic rubber, synthetic
petrol Biology — Test-Tube-babies artificial insemination

of animals, better breeds of hens, animals, biological drugs like hormones. Transport faster trains, aeroplanes, hovercraft, Jumbo-jets more efficient motorcars etc. Atomic science — bombs, atomic engines, atomic generators of electricity etc. Such wonders never seen before in human history.

49.*Jhe future of religion*

Begin by a review of the past — religion given greatest importance in the west and the east — The reaction from the 18 the century in the west — In India it began in late 19th century scientific discoveries cast doubt on the truths of the Bible and the creation of the world and of man. India, the stories of miracles and the religious system of castes being questioned — Idol worship being questioned — tendency towards atheism in the 20th century — Younger generation more inciined to show disregard to religion — in the west and in the east — among Christains and Hindus— not so is Islam or Jewish religions — A reaction to it now showing — The principles of religion being accepted but not the miracles or strict rules — the future — a loose free type of religion based on the good of society without religious intolerance or strict formalities.

50. *Js happiness possible even in modern times ?*

Two conflicting views — The optimistic — happiness possible now more than at any other times — comforts, conveniences, drugs, suregry, foods, new fabrics, better housing, better sanitation, better education, better jobs, more money, better entertainment like the cinema, radio, television, plays, concerts, better travels, quicker journeys by Rail and aeroplanes etc international social contacts.

The pessimists — terrible fear of the atomic and hydrogen bombs — umemployment, insecurity of life and property, poverty break up of family life, old people left uncared for new dangers of cancer, heart*— attacks, high blood pressure, noise and pollution of air. No peace or rest. Break up of family life and of marriage

Conclusion — Real happiness a state of mind and not of possession. Contentment true happiness — if that is present one can be happy under any circumstances — if not under none.

■　■　■

www.ingramcontent.com/pod-product-compliance
Lightning Source LLC
LaVergne TN
LVHW090052180726
843489LV00002B/597